Mmmm... Salads

Mmmm...
Salads

First published in 2011
Love Food is an imprint of Parragon Books Ltd

Parragon
Queen Street House
4 Queen Street
Bath BA1 1HE, UK

Copyright © Parragon Books Ltd 2011

ISBN: 978-1-4454-2445-3

Printed in China

Cover photography by Mike Cooper
Food styling by Lincoln Jefferson
Internal design by Talking Design
Introduction by Linda Doeser

Notes for the Reader
This book uses imperial, metric, and US cup measurements. Follow the same units of
measurement throughout; do not mix imperial and metric. All spoon measurements are
level: teaspoons are assumed to be 5 ml, and tablespoons are assumed to be 15 ml. Unless
otherwise stated, milk is assumed to be whole, eggs and individual vegetables, such as
potatoes, are medium, and pepper is freshly ground black pepper.

The times given are an approximate guide only. Preparation times differ according to the
techniques used by different people and the cooking times may also vary from those
given as a result of the type of oven used. Optional ingredients, variations, or serving
suggestions have not been included in the calculations.

Recipes using raw or very lightly cooked eggs should be avoided by infants, the elderly,
pregnant women, convalescents, and anyone with a chronic condition. Pregnant and
breast-feeding women are advised to avoid eating peanuts and peanut products.
People with nut allergies should be aware that some of the prepared ingredients used
in the recipes in this book may contain nuts. Always check the packaging before use.

contents

introduction

It is not news that governments and nutritionists in many countries have been recommending for a long time that we eat more fruit and vegetables—sometimes five a day, sometimes seven. Nor is it news that many adults and children in the Western world have been gaining too much weight and putting their health at risk. Nevertheless, it isn't always easy to make sure that the family eats healthily—life is busy, so shopping and cooking may sometimes take a back seat.

After-school activities and evening classes can lead to different mealtimes for different family members, making fast-food outlets appealing because they offer easy options. However, these often are not the healthiest choice. There is a better way. The recipes for salads in this book are so delicious and varied that five (or even seven) a day is made easy for the family cook to prepare and for everyone to eat and enjoy—even if family members have different tastes, with one not liking peas and another disliking carrots.

If you think of salad as simply being salad greens, cucumber, tomatoes, and some cold meat or grated cheese, you'll be really surprised by the irresistible array of tasty dishes in the following pages. There are no hard-and-fast rules about what makes a salad. Salad greens remain a popular choice, but other ingredients include fruit, such as strawberries and mango, legumes, such as lentils and lima beans, and vegetables, such as asparagus and bell peppers. Although we tend to think of salads as made from raw ingredients, cooked grains and beans are delicious additions and some of the most alluring salads are served warm.

top tips for success

• One of the keynotes of salads is texture. Limp greens will never become crisper with the addition of dressing, watery raw tomatoes are inedible, carrots must be crisp—not bendy—and avocados must be creamily ripe. Ingredients should be as fresh as possible, ideally prepared on the day of purchase. This is not just essential for taste and texture, but also for nutrition as many vitamins can be lost during storage.

• The variety of salad greens available these days is astonishing. There are 4 main types of lettuce: butterhead, crisphead, looseleaf and romaine, and of these there are many varieties, such as Bibb, Boston, iceberg, and oak leaf. Endive, frisée, and radicchio are all members of the chicory family and share a characteristic bitter flavor that peps up milder leaves. Arugula, young spinach leaves, and watercress also have a peppery taste that gives bite to mixed salads. Mâche, also known as lamb's lettuce and corn salad, is not a true lettuce but is a useful winter vegetable with a slightly nutty flavor. As well as combining sweet, mild, and peppery leaves for a delicious range of flavors, use a mixture of colors for visual appeal—we eat with our eyes as well as our mouths.

• Radishes are great for pepping up salads and adding color. There are many different varieties, the most popular being the small, round red ones and the red and white elongated French breakfast radishes. They are available all year round and are milder in the spring. Buy them with their leaves intact; if these are green and vigorous, it is an indication of freshness. Store them in the salad drawer of the refrigerator for up to 4 days.

• There are numerous varieties of tomatoes but not all are suited to salads. Cherry tomatoes, whether red or yellow, have a sweet flavor and appealing appearance. Children in particular like these miniatures. By contrast, beefsteak tomatoes may be as large as 4 inches/ 10 cm in diameter. They are usually ridged and may be deep red or orange. They have an excellent flavor and are ideal for salads. Slicing tomatoes are also known as salad tomatoes. However, some varieties have been carefully bred to withstand the handling of long transportation and storage and are rather insipid. Choose vine tomatoes to guarantee a richer taste and better texture. Store tomatoes in a bowl in the kitchen instead of in the refrigerator.

• Raw onions, particularly sweet, mild red, white, and Bermuda onions, add a delicious flavor to salads. If you are concerned about their astringency, soak them in salted water or sprinkle with salt and let stand for 15 minutes, then rinse well. Either dice finely or cut into wafer-thin slices. Scallions are a traditional ingredient in mixed salads. Both the white bulbs and the green tops may be used. Store scallions in the salad drawer of the refrigerator and other onions in a cool, dry place.

• Cucumbers may be smooth or ridged and are available in a range of lengths. It's a matter of personal taste whether you peel them but if you don't, wash them thoroughly as they are often given a wax coating to make them shiny. You can use a citrus stripper to cut narrow grooves in the peel so that when the cucumber is sliced it has an attractive scalloped edge. Always slice cucumber as thinly as possible. Store in the salad drawer of the refrigerator for up to 1 week. If it has a plastic cover, remove this completely before using.

• New potatoes are small, waxy potatoes that are not only delicious with mayonnaise and chives in a classic potato salad, but are also delicious in warm salads partnered with bacon or sausage. Any variety of young potato can be harvested as a new potato. Store them in a cool, dark, airy place.

• Avocados have to be picked before they ripen, otherwise they immediately fall off the tree. Buy them a few days before you intend to use them and let stand at room temperature for 4–5 days. When ripe, the fruit will "give" slightly when gently squeezed but will not feel soft. Do not let the skin develop dark patches. If you need to store the ripe avocado for a little longer, put it into the refrigerator.

• Celery is ideal for adding flavor and bulk to salads. It has a crunchy texture and distinctive flavor that is perfect for most salads. It has become a common household staple along with potatoes. Choose celery heads with leaves that look bright green and fresh. The leaves can also be used in salads and as a garnish. Store in a plastic bag or plastic wrap to prevent the stalks from going limp.

herb vinaigrette

makes about ⅔ cup
- ½ cup olive oil
- 3 tbsp white wine vinegar or lemon juice
- 1½ tbsp chopped fresh herbs, such as chives, parsley, or mint
- 1 tsp Dijon mustard
- ½ tsp superfine sugar
- salt and pepper

1 Put all the ingredients in a screw-top jar, secure the lid, and shake well until a thick emulsion forms. Taste, and adjust the seasoning if necessary.

2 Use immediately or store in an airtight container in the refrigerator for up to 3 days. Always whisk or shake the dressing again before using.

basil, chive & lemon dressing

serves 4–6
- 1 tbsp fresh dill, chopped
- 20 chives, snipped
- 4 tbsp basil, chive, and lemon vinegar
- 1 tsp Dijon mustard
- 2 tbsp olive oil
- 1 tbsp fresh lemon juice
- salt and pepper

1 Put the dill and chives in a mixing bowl and combine.

2 Whisk together the vinegar, mustard, oil, and lemon juice. Season to taste with salt and pepper and pour into the mixing bowl with the dill and chives.

3 Serve immediately or store, covered, in the refrigerator and bring to room temperature before serving.

garlic, chile & oregano oil

makes 1 cup

- 5 garlic cloves, halved lengthwise
- 2 tbsp seeded and chopped red hot chile
- 1 tsp dried oregano
- 1 cup canola oil

1 Preheat the oven to 300°F/150°C. Combine the garlic, chile, and oregano with the oil in an ovenproof glass measuring pitcher. Place on a glass pie plate in the center of the oven and heat for 1½–2 hours.

2 Remove from the oven, let cool, then strain through cheesecloth into a clean jar. Store, covered, in the refrigerator. You can also leave the garlic and chile pieces in the oil and strain before using.

tomato dressing

serves 2–4

- 2 tbsp balsamic vinegar, or red or white wine vinegar
- 4–6 tbsp extra virgin olive oil
- 1 tsp Dijon mustard
- pinch of superfine sugar
- 1 tbsp torn fresh basil leaves
- 1 tbsp chopped sun-dried tomatoes
- salt and pepper

1 Place all the ingredients in a screw-top jar, secure the top, and shake well. Alternatively, beat all the ingredients together in a small bowl. Use as much oil as you like.

2 If you have just salad greens to dress, 4 tablespoons of oil will be sufficient, but if you have heavier ingredients, such as potatoes, you will need about 6 tablespoons of oil.

3 Use the dressing immediately. If you want to store it, do not add the herbs — it will then keep for 3–4 days in the refrigerator.

Mmmm...
meat

roast beef salad

serves 4

- 1 lb 10 oz/750 g beef tenderloin, trimmed of any visible fat
- 2 tsp Worcestershire sauce
- 3 tbsp olive oil
- 3½ cups halved green beans
- 3½ oz/100 g dried orecchiette (ear-shaped pasta)
- 2 red onions, finely sliced
- 1 large head radicchio
- generous ¼ cup green olives, pitted
- scant ⅓ cup shelled, whole hazelnuts
- pepper

dressing

- 1 tsp Dijon mustard
- 2 tbsp white wine vinegar
- 5 tbsp olive oil

1 Preheat the oven to 425°F/220°C. Rub the beef with pepper to taste and Worcestershire sauce. Heat 2 tablespoons of the oil in a small roasting pan over high heat, add the beef, and sear on all sides. Transfer the dish to the preheated oven and roast for 30 minutes. Remove and let cool. Cut into thin slices.

2 Bring a large pan of water to a boil, add the beans, and cook for 5 minutes, or until just tender. Remove with a slotted spoon, keeping the cooking water, and refresh the beans under cold running water. Drain and put into a large bowl.

3 Return the bean cooking water to a boil, add the pasta, and cook for 12 minutes, or until tender but still firm to the bite. Drain, return to the pan, and toss with the remaining oil.

4 Add the pasta to the beans with the onions, radicchio leaves, olives, and hazelnuts, mix gently, and transfer to a serving bowl. Arrange some thinly sliced beef on top.

5 Whisk together all of the dressing ingredients in a separate bowl, then pour over the salad and serve at once with extra sliced beef.

warm beef salad niçoise

serves 4

- 4 tenderloin steaks, about 4 oz/115 g each, trimmed of any visible fat
- 2 tbsp red wine vinegar
- 2 tbsp orange juice
- 2 tsp prepared English mustard
- 2 eggs
- 6 oz/175 g new potatoes
- ¾ cup trimmed green beans
- 4–6 cups mixed salad greens, such as baby spinach, arugula, and mizuna
- 1 yellow bell pepper, seeded, peeled, and cut into strips
- 12 cherry tomatoes, halved
- black olives, pitted (optional)
- 2 tsp extra virgin olive oil

1 Place the steaks in a shallow dish. Blend the vinegar with 1 tablespoon of orange juice and 1 teaspoon of mustard. Pour over the steaks, cover, then let stand in the refrigerator for at least 30 minutes. Turn over halfway through the marinating time. Place the eggs in a pan and cover with cold water. Bring to a boil, then reduce the heat to a simmer and cook for 10 minutes. Remove and plunge the eggs into cold water. Once cold, shell and set aside. Meanwhile, place the potatoes in a pan and cover with cold water. Bring to a boil, then cover and let simmer for 15 minutes, or until tender when pierced with a fork. Drain and set aside.

2 Bring a saucepan of water to a boil, add the beans, and cook for 5 minutes, or until just tender. Drain, plunge into cold water, and drain again. Arrange the potatoes and beans on top of the salad greens together with the bell pepper, cherry tomatoes, and olives, if using. Blend the remaining orange juice and mustard with the olive oil and set aside. Heat a stove-top grill pan or griddle until smoking. Drain the steaks and cook for 3–5 minutes on each side or according to personal preference. Slice the steaks and arrange on top of the salad, then pour over the dressing and serve.

beef satay salad

serves 4

- 2 porterhouse steaks, each
  weighing about 8 oz/225 g
- 2 tbsp soy sauce
- 1 tbsp lime juice
- 1 garlic clove, crushed
- 1 tsp dried chili flakes
- 3¾ cups shredded
  Chinese cabbage
- ¼ cucumber, thinly sliced
- 4 scallions, sliced
- fresh cilantro leaves and
  sliced red chile, to garnish
- lime wedges, to serve

satay dressing

- 2 tbsp chunky peanut butter
- 3 tbsp coconut milk
- 1 tbsp soy sauce
- 1 tbsp lime juice
- 2 tsp brown sugar

1 Put the steaks into a shallow dish. Combine the soy sauce, lime juice, garlic, and chili flakes and pour the mixture over the steaks. Cover and let marinate at room temperature for 1 hour.

2 Heat a cast-iron grill pan until very hot. Add the steaks and cook for 3–5 minutes on each side, depending on how well done you like your steak. Transfer the steaks to a plate, cover, and let rest for 5 minutes.

3 To make the dressing, put all the ingredients into a small pan and heat gently, stirring continuously, until the peanut butter has melted. Simmer for 1 minute. If the dressing becomes too thick, add a little water and stir well to make a pouring consistency.

4 Combine the Chinese cabbage, cucumber, and scallions and put them on a serving platter. Thinly slice the steaks and arrange them on top of the salad. Drizzle the satay dressing over them and garnish with cilantro leaves and chile slices. Serve with lime wedges.

steak waldorf salad

serves 4
- 2 tenderloin steaks, about 6 oz/175 g each and 1 inch/2.5 cm thick
- olive or corn oil, for brushing
- 1 tbsp whole-grain mustard
- ⅔ cup mayonnaise
- 1 tbsp lemon juice
- 1 lb 2 oz/500 g apples
- 4 celery stalks, thinly sliced
- ½ cup walnut halves, broken into pieces
- 4 cups mixed salad greens
- pepper
- fresh whole wheat bread, to serve

1 Heat a cast-iron grill pan or heavy-bottom skillet over medium heat. Brush each steak with oil and season to taste with pepper. Add the steaks to the pan and cook for 6–7 minutes for rare or 8–10 minutes for medium, turning the steaks frequently and brushing once or twice with oil. Remove from the pan and set aside.

2 Meanwhile, stir the mustard into the mayonnaise. Put the lemon juice into a large bowl. Peel and core the apples, then cut them into small chunks and immediately toss in the lemon juice. Stir in the mustard mayonnaise. Add the celery and walnuts to the apple mixture and toss together.

3 Arrange the salad greens on 4 plates, then divide the apple mixture among them. Very thinly slice the steaks, arrange on top of the salads, and serve immediately with bread.

rare beef pasta salad

serves 4
- 1 lb/450 g porterhouse steak in 1 piece
- 1 lb/450 g dried fusilli (pasta spirals)
- 4 tbsp olive oil
- 2 tbsp lime juice
- 2 tbsp Thai fish sauce
- 2 tsp honey
- 4 scallions, sliced
- 1 cucumber, peeled and cut into 1-inch/2.5-cm chunks
- 3 tomatoes, cut into wedges
- 3 tsp finely chopped fresh mint
- salt and pepper

1 Season the steak with salt and pepper. Broil or pan-fry the steak for about 4 minutes on each side. Let stand for 5 minutes, then slice thinly across the grain and reserve until required.

2 Meanwhile, bring a large pan of lightly salted water to a boil over medium heat. Add the pasta and cook for 8–10 minutes, or according to the package directions, until tender but still firm to the bite. Drain thoroughly, then refresh in cold water and drain again. Return the pasta to the pan and toss in the oil.

3 Mix the lime juice, fish sauce, and honey together in a small pan and cook over medium heat for about 2 minutes.

4 Add the scallions, cucumber, tomatoes, and chopped mint to the pan, then add the steak and mix well. Season with salt to taste.

5 Transfer the pasta to a large, warmed serving dish and top with the steak mixture. Serve just warm or let cool completely.

beef salad with noodles

serves 4

- 12 oz/350 g porterhouse steak, trimmed of any visible fat
- 3½ oz/90 g egg noodles
- 1 small red onion, halved and thinly sliced
- 6 radishes, sliced
- 4 good handfuls of peppery leaves, such as tatsoi, mustard greens, and arugula
- 1½ tbsp peanut oil
- 1 tsp Sichuan pepper, crushed

marinade

- 4 tsp Chinese rice wine or dry sherry
- ½ tbsp soy sauce
- 4 tsp sugar
- 2 tbsp hoisin sauce
- 1-inch/2.5-cm piece fresh ginger, squeezed in a garlic press

dressing

- 2 tsp Sichuan pepper, crushed
- 1½ tbsp light soy sauce
- 1½ tbsp rice vinegar
- 2 tbsp cold-pressed sesame oil

1 Slice the beef into 1½-inch/4-cm wide strips. Combine all the marinade ingredients and pour over the beef. Marinate at room temperature for 30 minutes, or in the refrigerator for up to 2 days.

2 Cook the noodles according to the package directions and let cool. Snip into shorter lengths. Whisk all the dressing ingredients together until well blended. Combine the noodles, onion, radishes, and peppery leaves in a large bowl. Whisk the dressing again and pour two-thirds of it over the salad. Toss to distribute the noodles, then divide among individual serving plates.

3 Heat a wok over medium–high heat, then add the peanut oil and Sichuan pepper. Stir for a few seconds to flavor the oil. Add the beef and marinade and stir-fry for 4–5 minutes, until caramelized. Remove with a slotted spoon and scatter over the salad. Pour over the remaining dressing.

hot & sour beef salad

serves 4

- 1 tsp black peppercorns
- 1 tsp coriander seeds
- 1 dried red bird chile
- ¼ tsp Chinese five-spice powder
- 9 oz/250 g beef tenderloin
- 1 tbsp dark soy sauce
- 6 scallions
- 1 carrot
- ¼ cucumber
- 8 radishes
- 1 red onion
- ¼ head napa cabbage
- 2 tbsp peanut oil
- 1 garlic clove, crushed
- 1 tsp finely chopped lemongrass
- 1 tbsp chopped fresh mint
- 1 tbsp chopped fresh cilantro

dressing

- 3 tbsp lime juice
- 1 tbsp light soy sauce
- 2 tsp light brown sugar
- 1 tsp sesame oil

1 Crush the peppercorns, coriander seeds, and chile in a mortar with a pestle, then mix with the five-spice powder and sprinkle on a plate. Brush the beef all over with soy sauce, then roll it in the spices to coat evenly.

2 Cut the scallions into 2½-inch/6-cm lengths, then shred finely lengthwise. Place in ice water until curled. Drain well.

3 Trim the carrot and cut into very thin diagonal slices. Halve the cucumber, scoop out and discard the seeds, then slice the flesh thinly. Trim the radishes and cut into flower shapes.

4 Slice the onion thinly. Roughly shred the napa cabbage leaves. Toss all the vegetables together in a large salad bowl.

5 Heat the oil in a skillet and fry the garlic and lemongrass until golden. Add the beef and cook for 3–4 minutes, turning once. Remove from the heat.

6 Slice the beef thinly and toss into the salad with the mint and cilantro. Mix together the dressing ingredients and stir into the skillet, then spoon over the salad. Serve immediately.

broiled lamb salad

serves 4

- 2 tbsp sunflower oil, plus extra for brushing
- 1 tbsp tomato paste
- ½ tbsp ground cumin
- 1 tsp lemon juice
- 1 garlic clove, crushed
- pinch of cayenne pepper
- 1 lb 2 oz/500 g lamb neck fillets, trimmed of any visible fat
- salt and pepper
- toasted sesame seeds and chopped fresh flat-leaf parsley, to garnish

dressing

- 2 tbsp fresh lemon juice
- 1 tsp honey
- ⅓ cup thick plain yogurt
- 2 tbsp finely shredded fresh mint
- 2 tbsp chopped fresh flat-leaf parsley
- 1 tbsp finely snipped fresh chives
- salt and pepper

1 Mix together the oil, tomato paste, cumin, lemon juice, garlic, cayenne, and salt and pepper to taste in a nonmetallic bowl. Add the lamb and rub all over with the marinade. Cover the bowl and marinate in the refrigerator for at least 2 hours, but ideally overnight.

2 Meanwhile, to make the dressing, whisk the lemon juice and honey together until the honey dissolves. Whisk in the yogurt until well blended. Stir in the herbs and add salt and pepper to taste. Cover and chill until required.

3 Remove the lamb from the refrigerator 15 minutes before you are ready to cook. Heat the broiler to its highest setting and lightly brush the broiler rack with oil. Broil the lamb, turning it once, for 10 minutes for medium and 12 minutes for well done. Let the lamb cool completely, then cover and chill until required.

4 Thinly slice the lamb, then divide among 4 plates. Adjust the seasoning in the dressing, if necessary, then spoon over the lamb slices. Sprinkle with toasted sesame seeds and parsley and serve.

lamb kofte & herb salad

serves 4

- 12 oz/350 g lean ground lamb
- 1 small onion, finely chopped
- 2 tsp each ground coriander, ground cumin, and paprika
- 1 tbsp chopped fresh cilantro
- 2 tbsp chopped fresh mint
- 3 tbsp olive oil
- 6 tbsp plain yogurt
- 2½-inch-/5-cm piece cucumber, grated
- 2 tsp mint sauce
- 4 cups mixed baby leaf and herb salad
- 1 tbsp lemon juice
- salt and pepper

1 Put 8 wooden skewers into a shallow bowl of cold water and let soak for 30 minutes. Put the lamb, onion, spices, cilantro, and mint into a food processor with plenty of salt and pepper. Process for 1–2 minutes, until finely ground. Transfer to a bowl, cover, and chill in the refrigerator for 30 minutes.

2 Preheat the broiler to high. Divide the mixture into 8. Wrap the mixture around the soaked wooden skewers to form oval shapes. Brush with a little of the oil and broil under the broiler, turning frequently, for 15–20 minutes, until cooked through.

3 Meanwhile, combine the yogurt, cucumber, and mint sauce in a small bowl and season with salt and pepper.

4 Put the salad greens into a large bowl. Whisk the rest of the oil with the lemon juice and season to taste. Pour the dressing over the salad greens and toss to coat. Serve the hot koftes, on or off the skewers, with the salad and cucumber-and-mint yogurt.

roasted pork & pumpkin salad

serves 4–6

- 1 small pumpkin, about 3½ lb/1.6 kg, seeded and cut in half
- 2 red onions, cut into wedges
- olive oil, for brushing
- ¾ cup trimmed and halved green beans
- 4¼ cups cubed, roasted pork (with any skin or rind removed)
- large handful fresh arugula leaves
- 3½ oz/100 g feta cheese, drained and crumbled
- 2 tbsp toasted pine nuts
- 2 tbsp chopped fresh flat-leaf parsley
- salt and pepper

vinaigrette

- 6 tbsp extra virgin olive oil
- 3 tbsp balsamic vinegar
- ½ tsp sugar
- ½ tsp Dijon, prepared English, or whole-grain mustard

1 Preheat the oven to 400°F/200°C. Cut the pumpkin halves into wedges about 1½ inches/4 cm wide. Very lightly brush the pumpkin and onion wedges with the olive oil, place in a roasting pan, and roast for 25–30 minutes, until the pumpkin and onions are tender but holding their shape.

2 Meanwhile, bring a small pan of salted water to a boil. Add the green beans and cook for 5 minutes, or until tender. Drain well and cool under cold running water to stop them from cooking further. Drain well and pat dry.

3 Remove the pumpkin and onion wedges from the oven as soon as they are tender-crisp and let cool completely. When the pumpkin is cool, peel and cut into bite-size pieces.

4 To make the vinaigrette, place all the ingredients in a screw-top jar and shake vigorously until they are well blended.

5 Put the pumpkin wedges, onions, beans, pork, arugula, feta, pine nuts, and parsley in a large bowl and gently toss together. Shake the vinaigrette again, pour over the salad, and gently toss. Divide among individual bowls and serve.

hoisin pork with ribbon salad

serves 4
- 1 lb/450 g pork tenderloin
- 3 tbsp hoisin sauce
- 3 medium carrots
- ½ cucumber
- 4 scallions, finely shredded
- 4 radishes, very thinly sliced
- 2 tbsp sesame seeds

dressing
- 2 tbsp toasted sesame oil
- 2 tbsp rice vinegar

1 Cut the pork tenderloin into 2 pieces and put them into a shallow dish. Pour the hoisin sauce over them, cover, and let marinate at room temperature for 1 hour. Preheat the oven to 375°F/190°C.

2 Put the pork on a wire rack set over a roasting pan filled halfway with water (this helps to keep the pork moist during cooking). Roast for 35–40 minutes, until the pork is cooked through and lightly charred in places. Let cool for 10 minutes.

3 Use a vegetable peeler to slice the carrots and cucumber into thin ribbons. Put them into a bowl and toss together with the scallions and radishes.

4 Heat a nonstick skillet and add the sesame seeds. Cook over medium heat for 3–4 minutes, until lightly toasted. Add to the salad. Whisk together the sesame oil and vinegar and pour half the dressing over the salad. Toss well to mix.

5 Slice the pork tenderloin and transfer to individual serving plates with the ribbon salad on the side. Drizzle the rest of the dressing over the pork and serve immediately.

pork & cucumber salad

serves 4

- 1 lb/450 g pork tenderloin, trimmed of any visible fat
- 6 scallions, halved lengthwise and sliced into 3
- 1 cucumber
- 4 handfuls shredded iceberg lettuce
- 1 cup cilantro leaves
- ½ cup mint leaves
- 4 tbsp lightly crushed dry-roast peanuts
- finely grated zest of 1 lime
- 1 tsp salt
- 1 tsp sugar
- 1 tbsp kechap manis, or dark soy sauce
- 1 tbsp peanut oil
- 2 tsp sesame oil

marinade

- 2 small fresh red chiles, seeded and finely chopped
- 4 tbsp sugar
- 3 tbsp Thai fish sauce
- 4 tbsp lime juice
- 4 tbsp rice vinegar

1 Thinly slice the pork. Cut each slice in half lengthwise. Put in a bowl with the scallions. Peel the cucumber, halve lengthwise, and scoop out the seeds. Thinly slice diagonally and put in a bowl.

2 Next, make the marinade. Using a large mortar and pestle, pound the chopped chiles and the sugar to a watery, red paste. Add the Thai fish sauce, lime juice, and rice vinegar, stirring to dissolve the sugar. Pour into a pitcher. Pour one-half over the pork and scallions and one-half over the cucumber. Marinate for 1 hour, then drain the cucumber and reserve its marinade.

3 Put the shredded lettuce, cilantro, and mint in a bowl and toss to mix. Divide among individual serving plates. Arrange the cucumber slices on top and dress with the reserved marinade.

4 Mix the nuts with the lime zest, salt, and sugar. Heat a wok over high heat, then add the kechap manis and the oils. Stir-fry the pork for 5 minutes, until cooked through and slightly caramelized. Arrange the pork slices on top of the cucumber and sprinkle with the nut mixture. Serve at once.

hot sausage & potato salad

serves 4
- 1 lb 9 oz/700 g new potatoes, halved
- 1 tbsp sunflower oil
- 6 thick pork sausages
- 2 onions, sliced into thin wedges

dressing
- 4 tbsp olive oil
- 1 tbsp white wine vinegar
- 2 tsp whole-grain mustard
- 2 tsp honey
- salt and pepper

1 Bring a large pan of lightly salted water to a boil. Add the potatoes and cook for 12–15 minutes, or until just tender.

2 Meanwhile, heat the sunflower oil in a large skillet and cook the sausages for 5 minutes. Add the onions to the skillet and continue cooking, turning frequently, for another 8–10 minutes, until the sausages are cooked through and the onions are golden and tender. Remove the onions and sausages from the skillet and drain on paper towels. Slice each sausage diagonally into 4 pieces.

3 Drain the potatoes and put them into a large bowl with the onions and sausages.

4 To make the dressing, place all the ingredients in a screw-top jar and shake vigorously until they are well blended. Pour the dressing over the hot salad and toss well to coat. Adjust the seasoning to taste. Serve immediately.

spicy sausage pasta salad

serves 4
- 4½ oz/125 g dried conchiglie (pasta shells)
- 2 tbsp olive oil
- 1 medium onion, chopped
- 2 garlic cloves, finely chopped
- 1 small yellow bell pepper, seeded and cut into thin sticks
- 6 oz/175 g spicy pork sausage, such as chorizo or pepperoni, skinned and sliced
- 2 tbsp red wine
- 1 tbsp red wine vinegar
- 4 cups mixed salad greens
- salt

1 Bring a large pan of lightly salted water to a boil. Add the pasta and return to a boil. Cook for 8–10 minutes, or according to the package directions, until tender, but still firm to the bite. Drain and set aside.

2 Heat the oil in a pan over medium heat. Add the onion and cook until translucent, then stir in the garlic, yellow bell pepper, and sausage and cook for 3–4 minutes, stirring once or twice.

3 Add the wine, vinegar, and reserved pasta to the pan, stir, and bring the mixture just to a boil over medium heat. Drain.

4 Arrange the salad greens on serving plates, spoon over the warm sausage-and-pasta mixture, and serve immediately.

artichoke & chorizo salad

serves 8
- 12 small globe artichokes
- juice of ½ lemon
- 2 tbsp Spanish olive oil
- 1 small orange-flesh
- 7 oz/200 g cooked chorizo, outer casing removed
- fresh tarragon or flat-leaf parsley sprigs, to garnish

dressing
- 3 tbsp extra virgin olive oil
- 1 tbsp red wine vinegar
- 1 tsp prepared mustard
- 1 tbsp chopped fresh tarragon
- salt and pepper

1 Prepare the artichokes, then brush with lemon juice to prevent discoloration. Carefully remove the choke (the mass of silky hairs) by pulling it out with your fingers or by scooping it out with a spoon. Cut the artichokes into fourths and brush them again with lemon juice.

2 Heat the olive oil in a large, heavy-bottom skillet. Add the prepared artichokes and cook, stirring frequently, for 5 minutes, or until the artichoke leaves are golden brown. Remove from the skillet, then transfer to a large serving bowl and let cool.

3 To prepare the melon, cut in half and scoop out the seeds with a spoon. Cut the flesh into bite-size cubes. Add to the cooled artichokes. Cut the chorizo into bite-size chunks and add to the melon and artichokes.

4 To make the dressing, whisk the dressing ingredients together in a separate bowl. Just before serving, pour the dressing over the prepared salad ingredients and toss together. Serve the salad garnished with tarragon.

onion & herb salad with chorizo

serves 2
- 1 tbsp corn oil
- 1 small onion, finely sliced
- 9 oz/250 g canned lima beans, drained and rinsed
- 1 tsp balsamic vinegar
- 2 chorizo, sliced diagonally
- 1 small tomato, diced
- 2 tbsp harissa paste
- 3 cups mixed herb salad

1 Heat the oil in a nonstick skillet over medium heat, add the onion, and cook, stirring frequently, until softened but not browned. Add the beans and cook for an additional 1 minute, then add the vinegar, stirring well. Keep warm.

2 Meanwhile, heat a separate dry skillet over medium heat, add the chorizo slices, and cook, turning occasionally, until lightly browned. Remove with a slotted spoon and drain on paper towels.

3 Mix the tomato and harissa paste together in a small bowl. Divide the herb salad between 2 plates, spoon over the bean mixture, and sprinkle over the warm sausage slices. Top with a spoonful of the tomato-and-harissa mixture and serve at once.

warm bacon & egg salad

serves 4
- 2 romaine lettuce hearts, coarsely torn
- 4 eggs
- 2 tbsp sunflower oil
- 2 thick slices of bread, crusts removed and cubed
- 1⅓ cups cubed smoked bacon
- 12 cherry tomatoes, halved

dressing
- 2 tbsp extra virgin olive oil
- 1 tbsp red wine vinegar
- 1 tsp Dijon mustard
- pepper

1 To make the dressing, put all the ingredients into a small screw-top jar and shake until well blended. Put the lettuce leaves in a salad bowl.

2 Place the eggs in a saucepan and cover with cold water. Bring to the boil and boil for 4 minutes. Drain and plunge the eggs into cold water for 2 minutes. Peel off the shells and cut into quarters.

3 To make croutons, heat the sunflower oil in a large skillet and fry the bread cubes for 3–4 minutes, turning frequently until golden brown. Remove with a slotted spoon and set aside.

4 Add the bacon cubes to the pan and fry over medium–high heat until crisp and golden. Add the tomatoes and dressing to the pan and cook for an additional minute.

5 Gently toss the bacon, tomatoes, and dressing into the salad leaves. Add the quartered eggs and scatter over the croutons. Serve immediately.

bacon, lettuce & tomato salad

serves 4
- 8 thick slices lean bacon
- 1 iceberg lettuce, cut into 12 wedges
- 2 beefsteak tomatoes, sliced into wedges
- ¼ cucumber, thickly sliced
- ½ ripe avocado, peeled, pitted, and sliced
- 1 tbsp lemon juice
- ¾ cup coarsely grated cheddar cheese (optional)

dressing
- 4 tbsp mayonnaise
- 2 tbsp sour cream
- 1 tbsp milk
- 2 tsp whole-grain mustard
- salt and pepper

1 Preheat the broiler to high. Put the bacon slices on the broiler pan and broil for 3–4 minutes, turning once, until crisp.

2 To make the dressing, whisk the dressing ingredients together in a bowl.

3 Divide the lettuce wedges among 4 serving plates with the tomatoes and cucumber. Toss the avocado slices in the lemon juice and add to the salads.

4 Drizzle the dressing over the salads. Halve the bacon slices and stack them on top of the salads. Sprinkle the grated cheese over them, if using, and serve immediately.

spinach & bacon salad

serves 4
- 4 tbsp olive oil
- 4 slices lean bacon, diced
- 1 slice thick white bread, crusts removed, cut into cubes
- 1 lb/450 g fresh spinach, torn or shredded

1 Heat 2 tablespoons of the olive oil over high heat in a large skillet. Add the diced bacon to the skillet and cook for 3–4 minutes, or until crisp. Remove with a slotted spoon, draining carefully, and set aside.

2 To make croutons, toss the cubes of bread in the fat remaining in the skillet over high heat for about 4 minutes, or until crisp and golden. Remove the croutons with a slotted spoon, draining carefully, and set them aside.

3 Add the remaining oil to the skillet and heat. Toss the spinach in the oil over high heat for about 3 minutes, or until it has just wilted. Turn into a serving bowl and sprinkle with the bacon and croutons. Serve immediately.

walnut, pear & crispy bacon salad

serves 4
- 4 slices lean bacon
- scant ½ cup walnut halves
- 2 Red Bartlett pears, cored and sliced lengthwise
- 1 tbsp lemon juice
- 2 bunches watercress, tough stalks removed

dressing
- 3 tbsp extra virgin olive oil
- 2 tbsp lemon juice
- ½ tsp honey
- salt and pepper

1 Preheat the broiler to high. Put the bacon slices on the broiler pan and broil for 3–4 minutes, turning once, until crisp. Let cool, then cut into ½-inch/1-cm pieces.

2 Meanwhile, heat a dry skillet over medium heat and lightly toast the walnuts, shaking the skillet frequently, for 3 minutes, or until lightly browned. Let cool.

3 Toss the pears in the lemon juice to prevent discoloration. Put the watercress, walnuts, pears, and bacon into a salad bowl.

4 To make the dressing, whisk the dressing ingredients together in a separate bowl. Pour over the salad, toss well to combine, and serve.

artichoke &
prosciutto salad

serves 4

- 9¾ oz/275 g canned artichoke hearts in oil, drained
- 4 small tomatoes
- ¼ cup sun-dried tomatoes in oil, drained
- 1½ oz/40 g prosciutto
- 1 tbsp pitted and halved black olives
- handful of fresh basil sprigs
- fresh crusty bread, to serve

dressing

- 3 tbsp olive oil
- 1 tbsp white wine vinegar
- 1 garlic clove, crushed
- ½ tsp mild mustard
- 1 tsp honey
- salt and pepper

1 Make sure the artichoke hearts are thoroughly drained, then cut them into quarters and place in a serving bowl. Cut each tomato into wedges. Slice the sun-dried tomatoes into thin strips. Cut the prosciutto into thin strips and add to the bowl with the tomatoes and olive halves.

2 Keeping a few basil sprigs whole for garnishing, tear the remainder of the leaves into small pieces and add to the bowl containing the other salad ingredients.

3 To make the dressing, place all the ingredients in a screw-top jar and shake vigorously until they are well blended.

4 Pour the dressing over the salad and toss together. Garnish the salad with a few basil sprigs and serve with crusty bread.

prosciutto with melon & asparagus

serves 4
- 8 oz/225 g asparagus spears
- 1 small or ½ medium Galia or cantaloupe melon
- 2 oz/55 g prosciutto, thinly sliced
- 5½ cups package mixed salad greens, such as herb salad with arugula
- generous ½ cup fresh raspberries
- 1 tbsp freshly shaved Parmesan cheese
- salt

dressing
- 1 tbsp balsamic vinegar
- 2 tbsp raspberry vinegar
- 2 tbsp orange juice

1 Trim the asparagus, cutting in half if very long. Cook in lightly salted boiling water over medium heat for 5 minutes, or until tender. Drain and plunge into cold water, then drain again and set aside.

2 Cut the melon in half and scoop out the seeds. Cut into small wedges and cut away the rind. Separate the prosciutto slices, cut in half, and wrap around the melon wedges.

3 Arrange the salad greens on a large serving platter, place the asparagus spears alongside them, and top the spears with the melon wedges.

4 Scatter over the raspberries and Parmesan cheese shavings. To make the dressing, place all the ingredients in a screw-top jar and shake vigorously until they are well blended. Pour over the salad and serve.

spinach &
pancetta salad

serves 4
- generous 6 cups fresh baby spinach leaves
- 2 tbsp olive oil
- 5½ oz/150 g pancetta, cubed
- 10 oz/280 g mixed wild mushrooms, sliced

dressing
- 5 tbsp olive oil
- 1 tbsp balsamic vinegar
- 1 tsp Dijon mustard
- pinch of sugar
- salt and pepper

1 To make the dressing, whisk the dressing ingredients together in a bowl. Rinse the baby spinach under cold running water, then drain and place in a large salad bowl.

2 Heat the oil in a large skillet. Add the pancetta and cook for 3 minutes. Add the mushrooms and cook for 3–4 minutes, or until tender.

3 Pour the dressing into the skillet and immediately turn the cooked mixture and dressing into the bowl with the spinach. Toss until coated with the dressing and serve at once.

pastrami & bell pepper antipasti salad

serves 4
- 1 iceberg lettuce
- 10 oz/280 g charbroiled bell pepper antipasto in oil
- 1 cup sun-dried tomatoes in oil
- 1 cup pitted green olives
- 4 oz/115 g wafer-thin pastrami slices
- fresh basil leaves, to garnish

dressing
- 2 tbsp balsamic vinegar
- 1 tsp Dijon mustard
- pinch of sugar
- salt and pepper

1 Tear the lettuce into small chunks and put them into a serving bowl. Drain the bell pepper antipasto and sun-dried tomatoes, reserving 4 tablespoons of the oil. Coarsely chop the bell peppers and tomatoes and toss into the lettuce with the olives.

2 To make the dressing, combine the reserved oil, the vinegar, mustard, and sugar in a separate bowl and season to taste with salt and pepper. Pour half the dressing over the salad and toss well to mix. Arrange the pastrami in ruffles on top of the salad. Serve drizzled with the rest of the dressing and garnished with basil leaves.

prosciutto & salami salad with figs

serves 6
- 6 ripe figs
- 6 thin slices prosciutto
- 12 thin slices salami
- 1 small bunch of fresh basil, separated into small sprigs
- a few fresh mint sprigs
- handful of arugula leaves

dressing
- 2 tbsp lemon juice
- 4 tbsp extra virgin olive oil
- salt and pepper

1 Trim the stems of the figs to leave just a short length, then cut the figs into quarters. Arrange the prosciutto and salami on a large serving platter.

2 Wash and dry the herbs and arugula and put in a bowl with the prepared figs. To make the dressing, whisk the lemon juice and oil together in a small bowl and season well with salt and pepper.

3 Pour the dressing into the bowl with the herbs, arugula, and figs. Toss carefully until all the ingredients are well coated in the dressing. Spoon the figs and salad on top of the meat on the serving platter. Serve immediately.

salami pasta salad

serves 4–6

- 12 oz/350 g dried penne (pasta quills)
- 2 tbsp pesto sauce
- 3 tbsp olive oil
- 1 orange bell pepper, seeded and diced
- 1 yellow bell pepper, seeded and diced
- 1 red onion, finely diced
- ¾ cup pitted black olives
- 6 cherry tomatoes, halved
- 6-oz/175-g piece Milano salami, cut into small chunks
- 4½ oz/125 g mozzarella cheese, torn into small pieces
- salt and pepper
- fresh basil sprigs, to garnish

1 Bring a large pan of lightly salted water to a boil. Add the pasta and return to a boil. Cook for 10–12 minutes, or according to the package directions, until just tender, but still firm to the bite.

2 Drain the pasta well and transfer to a bowl. Combine the pesto sauce and olive oil and stir the mixture into the hot pasta. Let cool, stirring occasionally.

3 Add the bell peppers, onion, olives, tomatoes, salami, and mozzarella cheese to the pasta and toss well to mix. Season to taste with salt and pepper. Serve garnished with the basil sprigs.

goat cheese salad with prosciutto

serves 4
- 4 just ripe peaches, halved, pitted, and cut into 6 slices
- 1 tbsp olive oil
- 2 tsp lemon juice
- 1 cup mâche
- 1 cup frisée
- 4½ oz/125 g mild goat cheese, crumbled
- 4 slices prosciutto
- 1 tbsp toasted hazelnuts, chopped
- salt and pepper

dressing
- 4 tbsp olive oil
- 2 tbsp hazelnut oil
- 2 tbsp red wine vinegar
- ½ tsp sugar
- salt and pepper

1 To make the dressing, whisk the dressing ingredients together in a bowl.

2 Place the peach slices in a separate bowl and add the olive oil and lemon juice. Turn to coat and season lightly with salt and pepper.

3 Heat a cast-iron grill pan and add the peach slices. Cook over medium heat for 2–3 minutes, turning once, until lightly charred and just starting to soften.

4 Mix the mâche and frisée together in a bowl and add half the dressing. Toss well to coat and divide among 4 serving plates. Top with the warm peach slices and crumbled goat cheese. Place a ruffled slice of prosciutto on the top of each salad.

5 Drizzle over the rest of the dressing and scatter over the toasted hazelnuts. Serve immediately.

Mmmm...
poultry

waldorf chicken salad

serves 4

- 4½ cups diced red apples
- 3 tbsp fresh lemon juice
- ⅔ cup light mayonnaise
- 1 head celery
- 4 shallots, sliced
- 1 garlic clove, finely chopped
- ¾ cup chopped walnuts, plus extra to garnish
- 3½ cups cubed, cooked chicken
- 1 romaine lettuce
- pepper

1 Place the apples in a bowl with the lemon juice and 1 tablespoon of mayonnaise. Let stand for 40 minutes.

2 Using a sharp knife, slice the celery very thinly. Add the celery, shallots, garlic, and walnuts to the apple and mix together. Stir in the remaining mayonnaise and blend thoroughly.

3 Add the cooked chicken to the bowl and mix well.

4 Line a serving dish with the lettuce. Pile the chicken salad into a serving bowl, sprinkle with pepper, and garnish with the chopped walnuts. Serve immediately.

creamy chicken salad

serves 4

- 1 tbsp sunflower oil
- 1 tbsp unsalted cashew nuts
- 1 tbsp whole blanched almonds
- 1 onion, chopped
- 1 tbsp mild curry paste
- 4 tbsp mayonnaise
- 4 tbsp plain yogurt
- 1 tbsp mango chutney
- 3¼ cups bite-size, cooked, skinless, boneless chicken pieces
- 5 cups watercress, spinach, and arugula salad
- 1 small mango, peeled, pitted, and sliced
- salt and pepper
- fresh cilantro leaves, to garnish

1 Heat the oil in a skillet. Add the cashew nuts and almonds and cook for 2–3 minutes, until golden. Remove with a slotted spoon and drain on paper towels.

2 Add the onion to the skillet and cook gently for 6–7 minutes, until softened and golden. Stir in the curry paste and cook for another minute. Transfer to a bowl and let cool.

3 Stir the mayonnaise, yogurt, and mango chutney into the onion and mix well. Add the cooked chicken pieces to the dressing. Toss well to coat. Season with salt and pepper.

4 Put the salad greens into a shallow serving bowl. Add the curried chicken and mango slices to the bowl and toss gently into the salad greens. Sprinkle the nuts over the salad and serve garnished with cilantro leaves.

braised chicken salad

serves 4
- 3 tbsp olive oil
- 1 chicken, weighing about 3 lb/1.3 kg
- scant 1 cup dry white wine
- 1 onion, chopped
- 1 carrot, chopped
- 1 celery stalk, chopped
- 1 fresh bay leaf
- salt and pepper

marinade
- 1 tsp black peppercorns
- 4 fresh bay leaves
- ½ cup olive oil
- salt

salad
- 5½ cups baby spinach leaves
- 5 tender celery stalks
- 1 head Belgian endive
- 1 tsp wine vinegar
- 1 tsp balsamic vinegar
- salt

1 Preheat the oven to 350°F/180°C. Heat the olive oil in a flameproof casserole over medium–high heat. Add the chicken and fry for 15 minutes, turning, until golden all over. Pour in the wine and simmer for 2 minutes, then add the remaining main ingredients. Cover tightly and transfer to the oven. Bake for 45–50 minutes, turning every 20 minutes, until the juices from the thickest part of the thigh run clear when pierced with a skewer. Discard the liquid and solids. When cool, remove and discard the skin. Strip the meat from the bone, slicing any large chunks into bite-size pieces.

2 Arrange the chicken in a dish to marinate. Sprinkle with a little salt, a few peppercorns, and the bay leaves. Pour in enough oil to generously coat. Cover tightly with plastic wrap and marinate in the refrigerator for 1–2 days. Remove the chicken from the refrigerator 2 hours before serving. Place in a colander set over a bowl to drain, and let stand until the oil has liquefied.

3 To make the salad, chop the leaves as desired. Combine the spinach, celery, and endive in a large serving dish. Toss with salt, enough oil from the chicken to just coat the leaves, and the wine vinegar. Arrange the chicken on top, discarding the peppercorns and bay leaves. Sprinkle with the balsamic vinegar before serving.

smoked chicken salad

serves 4–6

- 2 large, juicy tomatoes, sliced
- 1 lb 5 oz/600 g cooked, smoked chicken, skinned and cut into slices
- 3 bunches fresh watercress, any thick stems or yellow leaves removed, then rinsed and patted dry
- ¾ cup fresh bean sprouts, soaked for 20 minutes in cold water, then drained well and patted dry
- leaves from several sprigs fresh flat-leaf parsley or cilantro

dressing

- 1 ripe, soft avocado
- 2 tbsp lemon juice
- 1 tbsp tarragon vinegar
- ⅓ cup thick plain yogurt
- 1 small garlic clove, crushed
- 1 tbsp chopped fresh tarragon leaves
- salt and pepper

1 To make the dressing, put the avocado, lemon juice, and vinegar in a blender or food processor and blend until smooth, scraping down the side with a rubber spatula. Add the yogurt, garlic, and tarragon leaves and process again. Season with salt and pepper to taste, then transfer to a bowl. Cover closely with plastic wrap and chill for 2 hours.

2 To assemble the salad, divide the tomato slices among 4–6 individual plates. Toss the smoked chicken, watercress, bean sprouts, and parsley together. Divide the salad ingredients among the plates.

3 Adjust the seasoning in the dressing, if necessary. Spoon the dressing over each salad and serve.

roasted chicken with pesto cream salad

serves 4–6

- 4¼ cups cubed, cooked, skinless, boneless chicken
- 3 celery stalks, chopped
- 2 large, skinned red bell peppers from a jar, well drained and sliced
- salt and pepper
- iceberg lettuce, to serve

pesto cream

- ⅔ cup sour cream
- about 4 tbsp prepared pesto sauce

1 To make the pesto cream, put the sour cream into a large bowl, then beat in 4 tablespoons of the pesto sauce. Taste and add more pesto if you want a stronger flavor.

2 Add the chicken, celery, and bell peppers to the bowl. Season to taste with salt and pepper and toss well. Cover and chill until required.

3 Remove the salad from the refrigerator 10 minutes before serving to return to room temperature. Give the salad ingredients a good stir, then divide among individual plates lined with lettuce leaves.

chicken & pancetta caesar salad

serves 2

- 12 thin slices smoked pancetta
- 8 oz/225 g skinless, boneless chicken breasts, cubed
- 1 garlic clove, crushed
- 3 tbsp olive oil
- 1 small rustic or ciabatta roll, cut into chunky cubes
- 1 small romaine lettuce, chopped into large pieces
- fresh Parmesan cheese shavings, to serve

dressing

- 3 tbsp mayonnaise
- 2 tbsp sour cream
- 1 tbsp milk
- 1 small garlic clove, crushed
- ½ tsp Dijon mustard
- 2 tbsp finely grated Parmesan cheese
- 2 anchovy fillets in oil, drained and finely chopped
- pepper

1 To make the dressing, put all the ingredients into a food processor and process until smooth.

2 Heat a large nonstick skillet and add the pancetta slices. Cook over high heat for about 2 minutes, until crisp. Remove with a slotted spoon and drain on paper towels. Add the chicken to the skillet and cook over medium–high heat for 5–6 minutes, until golden and cooked through. Remove and drain with the pancetta.

3 To make garlic croutons, add the garlic and oil to the skillet and stir in the bread cubes. Cook over high heat, turning frequently, for 2–3 minutes, until crisp and golden.

4 Put the lettuce and dressing into a serving bowl and toss together thoroughly. Add the pancetta and chicken and toss in gently. Sprinkle with the garlic croutons and Parmesan cheese shavings and serve immediately.

honey & chicken pasta salad

serves 4
- 9 oz/250 g dried fusilli (pasta spirals)
- 2 tbsp olive oil
- 1 onion, thinly sliced
- 1 garlic clove, crushed
- 14 oz/400 g skinless, boneless chicken breasts, thinly sliced
- 2 tbsp whole-grain mustard
- 2 tbsp honey
- 10 cherry tomatoes, halved
- handful of mizuna or arugula leaves
- fresh thyme leaves, to garnish

dressing
- 3 tbsp olive oil
- 1 tbsp sherry vinegar
- 2 tsp honey
- 1 tbsp fresh thyme leaves
- salt and pepper

1 To make the dressing, whisk the dressing ingredients together in a bowl.

2 Bring a large pan of lightly salted water to a boil. Add the pasta and return to a boil. Cook for 10–12 minutes, or according to the package directions, until just tender.

3 Meanwhile, heat the oil in a large skillet. Add the onion and garlic and cook for 5 minutes. Add the chicken and cook, stirring frequently, for 3–4 minutes, until just cooked through. Stir the mustard and honey into the pan and cook for another 2–3 minutes, until the chicken and onion are golden brown and sticky.

4 Drain the pasta and transfer to a serving bowl. Pour the dressing over it and toss well. Stir in the chicken and onion and let cool.

5 Gently stir the tomatoes and mizuna into the pasta. Serve garnished with the thyme leaves.

chicken & cranberry salad

serves 4

- 1 cooked smoked chicken, weighing 3 lb/1.3 kg
- scant 1 cup dried cranberries
- 2 tbsp apple juice or water
- 3 cups sugar snap peas
- 2 ripe avocados
- juice of ½ lemon
- 4 lettuce hearts
- 1 bunch watercress, trimmed
- 2¾ cups arugula

dressing

- 2 tbsp olive oil
- 1 tbsp walnut oil
- 2 tbsp lemon juice
- 1 tbsp chopped fresh mixed herbs, such as parsley and lemon thyme
- salt and pepper

1 Carve the chicken carefully, slicing the white meat. Divide the legs into thighs and drumsticks and trim the wings. Cover with plastic wrap and refrigerate. Put the cranberries in a bowl. Stir in the apple juice, then cover with plastic wrap and let soak for 30 minutes.

2 Meanwhile, blanch the sugar snap peas in boiling water, then refresh under cold running water and drain. Peel, pit, and slice the avocados and toss in the lemon juice to prevent discoloration. Separate the lettuce hearts and arrange on a large serving platter with the avocados, sugar snap peas, watercress, arugula, and the chicken.

3 To make the dressing, place all the ingredients in a screw-top jar and shake vigorously until they are well blended. Drain the cranberries and mix them with the dressing, then pour over the salad. Serve immediately.

chicken & grapefruit salad

serves 4

- 2 skinless, boneless chicken breasts, about 6 oz/175 g each
- 1 bouquet garni
- few black peppercorns
- 2 pink grapefruits
- 3 Boston lettuce, separated into leaves
- 1 head Belgian endive, separated into leaves
- fresh chervil sprigs, to garnish

dressing

- 1 tbsp light olive oil
- 3 tbsp Greek-style yogurt
- 1 tsp whole-grain mustard
- pinch of sugar
- 1 tbsp chopped fresh chervil
- salt and pepper

1 Put the chicken into a large pan and pour in enough water to cover. Add the bouquet garni and peppercorns and bring to a gentle simmer. Cover and simmer for 25–30 minutes, until just cooked through. Let the chicken cool in the liquid.

2 Using a serrated knife, cut away the peel and pith from the grapefruits. Holding the fruit over a bowl to catch any juice, segment the flesh. Reserve 2 tablespoons of the juice.

3 Toss the salad greens in a bowl with the grapefruit segments.

4 To make the dressing, put all the ingredients into a bowl with the reserved grapefruit juice. Whisk together until thoroughly blended.

5 Drain the poached chicken and pat dry with paper towels. Tear into bite-size strips or thinly slice. Arrange on top of the salad. Drizzle with the dressing and season with a little more pepper to serve. Serve garnished with sprigs of fresh chervil.

chicken avocado salad

serves 4

- 4 large handfuls mixed salad greens, such as beet greens, escarole, endive, and radicchio rinsed and dried
- 3 cups cubed, cooked, skinless, boneless chicken
- 2 satsumas, separated into segments
- 2 celery stalks, thinly sliced
- ½ red onion, halved and thinly sliced
- 2 tbsp snipped fresh chives
- 2 avocados
- 2 tbsp toasted sunflower seeds, to garnish
- pita chips, to serve

dressing

- ½ cup extra virgin olive oil
- 3 tbsp Chinese rice wine vinegar
- ½ tsp Dijon mustard
- salt and pepper

1 To make the dressing, place all the ingredients in a screw-top jar and shake vigorously until they are well blended.

2 Put the salad greens into a bowl, add about one-third of the dressing, and lightly toss. Add the chicken, satsumas, celery, onion, chives, and the remaining dressing and toss again.

3 Cut the avocados in half and remove the pit, then peel away the skin. Cut the flesh into thin slices, add to the other ingredients, and gently toss together, making sure the avocado slices are completely coated with dressing so they don't discolor.

4 Arrange on individual plates, sprinkle with sunflower seeds, and serve with pita chips on the side.

cajun chicken salad

serves 4

- 4 skinless, boneless chicken breasts, about 5 oz/140 g each
- 4 tsp Cajun seasoning
- 2 tsp corn oil (optional)
- 1 ripe mango, peeled, pitted, and cut into thick slices
- 6 cups mixed salad greens
- 1 red onion, halved and thinly sliced
- 1 cup diced, cooked beet
- ¾ cup sliced radishes
- scant ½ cup walnut halves
- sesame seeds, to garnish

dressing

- 4 tbsp walnut oil
- 1–2 tsp Dijon mustard
- 1 tbsp lemon juice
- salt and pepper

1 Make 3 diagonal slashes across each chicken breast. Put the chicken into a shallow dish and sprinkle all over with the Cajun seasoning. Cover and let chill for at least 30 minutes.

2 When ready to cook, brush a stove-top grill pan with the corn oil, if using. Heat over high heat until very hot and a few drops of water sprinkled into the pan sizzle immediately. Add the chicken and cook for 7–8 minutes on each side, or until thoroughly cooked. If still slightly pink in the center, cook a little longer. Remove the chicken and set aside.

3 Add the mango slices to the pan and cook for 2 minutes on each side. Remove and set aside. Meanwhile, arrange the salad greens in a salad bowl and sprinkle over the onion, beet, radishes, and walnut halves.

4 To make the dressing, place all the ingredients in a screw-top jar and shake vigorously until they are well blended. Pour over the salad. Arrange the mango and the salad on the serving plate, top with the chicken breast, sprinkle with sesame seeds, and serve.

bbq chicken salad

serves 4

- 1 tbsp olive oil
- 4 tbsp tomato sauce
- 1 tbsp honey
- 1 tbsp Worcestershire sauce
- 1 tsp mustard powder
- 4 boneless chicken breasts (with skin), about 5 oz/140 g each
- 4 Boston lettuce, separated into leaves
- 4 carrots, coarsely grated
- ⅓ cup drained, canned corn kernels
- ½ red bell pepper, seeded and thinly sliced
- salt and pepper
- fresh chives, to garnish (optional)

dressing

- 6 tbsp sour cream
- 2 tbsp snipped fresh chives
- salt and pepper

1 Put the oil, tomato sauce, honey, Worcestershire sauce, and mustard powder into a shallow bowl and mix together well. Season with salt and pepper. Add the chicken and turn to coat in the marinade. Cover and let marinate in the refrigerator for 3–4 hours or overnight.

2 Preheat the barbecue. Drain the chicken, reserving the marinade. Cook the chicken over medium-hot coals, turning frequently and brushing with the reserved marinade, until thoroughly cooked. Let cool.

3 Divide the lettuce leaves among 4 serving plates. Sprinkle with the carrots, corn, and bell pepper. To make the dressing, combine the sour cream and snipped chives in a small bowl and season with salt and pepper.

4 Thickly slice each chicken portion and arrange on the salads. Serve with the sour cream dressing and garnish with fresh chives, if using.

chicken fajita salad

serves 4
- 1 lb/450 g skinless, boneless chicken breasts, sliced
- 2 tbsp lime juice
- 2 tbsp olive oil
- 1 tsp pepper
- 1 tsp dried oregano
- 1 tsp mild chili powder
- 1 onion, sliced into thin wedges
- 1 red bell pepper, seeded and thickly sliced
- 6 cups mixed salad greens
- lime slices and sour cream, to serve

avocado salsa
- 1 ripe avocado, peeled, pitted, and finely diced
- 2 ripe tomatoes, finely chopped
- 1 tbsp chopped fresh cilantro
- 1 tbsp lime juice
- salt and pepper

1 To make the avocado salsa, put the avocado into a small bowl and stir in the tomatoes, cilantro, and lime juice. Season with salt and pepper. Cover the surface closely with plastic wrap and chill in the refrigerator.

2 Put the chicken into a bowl. Add the lime juice, oil, pepper, oregano, and chili powder. Toss to coat. Cover and let marinate at room temperature for 1 hour.

3 Heat a cast-iron grill pan until very hot and add the chicken slices. Cook for 5–6 minutes, turning occasionally, until the chicken is cooked through and charred in places. Remove from the pan and keep warm. Add the onion and bell pepper to the pan and cook, turning once, for 3–4 minutes, until just tender.

4 Divide the salad greens among 4 serving plates and top with the chicken, onion, and bell pepper. Serve immediately with the avocado salsa, lime slices, and sour cream.

thai chicken salad

serves 6
- vegetable oil spray
- 4 oz/115 g skinless chicken breast, cut lengthwise horizontally
- 1 oz/25 g rice vermicelli
- store-bought low-fat spicy dressing of your choice
- 3 limes, halved

salad
- ½ cup thinly sliced, seeded mixed bell peppers
- ⅓ cup thin carrot strips
- ⅓ cup thin zucchini strips
- ⅓ cup thin snow pea strips
- scant ½ cup baby corn, sliced into thin strips
- ½ cup ¼-inch/5-mm broccoli floret pieces
- ½ cup shredded bok choy
- 4 tbsp coarsely chopped fresh cilantro leaves

1 Heat a grill pan over high heat and spray lightly with oil. Add the chicken and cook for 2 minutes on each side, or until thoroughly cooked through. Remove the chicken from the pan and shred.

2 Cook the vermicelli according to the package directions.

3 To make the salad, put all the salad ingredients with the chicken into a large bowl. Drain the vermicelli and add to the bowl. Pour the dressing over the salad and toss together, making sure that all the ingredients are well coated.

4 Cover and chill in the refrigerator for at least 2 hours before serving. Serve on large plates, squeezing the juice from half a lime over each serving.

chinese chicken salad

serves 4

- 3 skinless, boneless chicken breasts, weighing 1 lb/450 g in total, cut into bite-size pieces
- 2 tsp soy sauce
- ¼ tsp white pepper
- 2 tbsp peanut oil, plus extra for deep-frying
- 1¾ oz/50 g thin rice noodles
- ½ head Chinese cabbage, thinly sliced diagonally
- 3 scallions, green parts included, sliced diagonally
- ¼ cup almonds with skin, sliced lengthwise
- sesame seeds, to garnish (optional)

dressing

- 5 tbsp olive oil
- 3 tbsp rice vinegar
- 3 tbsp light soy sauce
- a few drops sesame oil
- salt and pepper

1 Sprinkle the chicken with the soy sauce and white pepper. To make the dressing, whisk the dressing ingredients together in a separate bowl.

2 Heat a wok over high heat, then add the peanut oil. Stir-fry the chicken for 4–5 minutes, until brown and crisp. Drain on paper towels and let cool. Wipe out the wok.

3 Pour enough peanut oil for deep-frying into the wok. Heat until almost smoking, then fry a few noodles at a time, until puffed up and crisp. Drain on paper towels.

4 Arrange the Chinese cabbage in a shallow serving dish. Place the noodles in a pile on top of the leaves, on one side of the dish. Arrange the chicken, scallions, and almonds in the remaining space. Whisk the dressing again and pour over the salad. Garnish with the sesame seeds, if using, and serve immediately.

gingered chicken & vegetable salad

serves 4

- 4 skinless, boneless chicken breasts
- 4 scallions, chopped
- 1-inch/2.5-cm piece fresh ginger, finely chopped
- 2 garlic cloves, crushed
- 2 tbsp vegetable oil or peanut oil

salad

- 1 tbsp vegetable oil or peanut oil
- 1 onion, sliced
- 2 garlic cloves, crushed
- 1 cup halved baby corn
- 1½ cups diagonally halved snow peas
- 1 red bell pepper, seeded and sliced
- 3-inch/7.5-cm piece cucumber, peeled, seeded, and sliced
- 4 tbsp Thai soy sauce
- 1 tbsp light brown sugar
- a few Thai basil leaves
- 6 oz/175 g fine egg noodles

1 Cut the chicken into 1-inch/2.5-cm cubes. Mix the scallions, ginger, crushed garlic, and 1 tablespoon of the oil together in a shallow dish. Add the chicken. Cover and let marinate for at least 3 hours. Lift the meat out of the marinade and set aside.

2 For the salad, heat a wok over medium heat, then add the oil. Add the onion and cook for 1–2 minutes, then add the garlic, baby corn, snow peas, and bell pepper. Cook for 2–3 minutes, until just tender. Add the cucumber, half the soy sauce, the sugar, and basil, and mix gently.

3 Cook the noodles according to the package directions, then drain well. Sprinkle the remaining soy sauce over them and arrange on plates. Top the noodles with the cooked vegetables.

4 Add the remaining oil to the wok and cook the chicken over fairly high heat, until browned on all sides. Arrange the chicken cubes on top of the salad and serve hot or warm.

101

turkey & peanut salad

serves 4
- 8 oz/225 g Chinese cabbage, coarsely torn
- 2 carrots, cut into thin sticks
- ½ cucumber, seeded and cut into thin sticks
- 1 cup bean sprouts
- 3 cups shredded, cooked, boneless turkey
- 1 tbsp toasted sesame seeds
- 1 tbsp chopped salted peanuts

dressing
- 4 tbsp smooth peanut butter
- 2 tbsp sweet chili sauce
- 1 tbsp soy sauce
- 1 tbsp rice vinegar
- 1 tbsp sunflower oil
- 1 tbsp roasted peanut oil

1 To make the dressing, put the peanut butter into a heatproof bowl. Set the bowl over a pan of simmering water and stir until the peanut butter has melted. Stir in the chili sauce, soy sauce, and rice vinegar. Remove from the heat and gradually stir in the sunflower and peanut oils to make a dressing with a smooth pouring consistency.

2 Put the Chinese cabbage leaves on a serving platter and top with the carrots, cucumber, and bean sprouts. Top with the shredded turkey and spoon the warm dressing over it. Sprinkle with the sesame seeds and peanuts and serve immediately.

turkey couscous salad

serves 4

- 1⅓ cups couscous
- 5 tbsp olive oil
- 3 tbsp red wine vinegar
- 12 oz/350 g turkey breast fillet, cubed
- 1 tsp harissa paste
- 1⅓ cups diced zucchini
- 1 onion, chopped
- ½ cup chopped dried apricots
- 2 tbsp toasted pine nuts
- 2 tbsp chopped fresh cilantro
- salt and pepper
- chopped fresh cilantro, to garnish

1 Put the couscous into a large heatproof bowl. Pour in enough boiling water to cover. Stir well, cover, and let soak for about 15 minutes, until all the liquid has been absorbed. Use a fork to break up any clumps and stir in 3 tablespoons of the olive oil and the vinegar. Season with plenty of salt and pepper.

2 Heat the remaining oil in a large skillet and add the turkey and harissa paste. Cook, turning frequently, for 3 minutes, until the turkey is no longer pink. Add the zucchini and onion to the skillet and cook, stirring occasionally, for another 10–12 minutes, until the turkey and vegetables are golden brown and tender.

3 Stir the turkey and vegetables into the couscous with the apricots and pine nuts. Let cool for 10 minutes, then stir in the chopped cilantro and adjust the seasoning to taste. Serve piled into bowls and garnished with chopped cilantro.

turkey & rice salad

serves 4

- 4 cups chicken stock
- scant 1 cup mixed long-grain and wild rice
- 2 tbsp corn oil
- 8 oz/225 g skinless, boneless turkey breast, trimmed of all visible fat and cut into thin strips
- 2 cups snow peas
- 4 oz/115 g oyster mushrooms, torn into pieces
- ¼ cup finely chopped, shelled pistachio nuts
- 2 tbsp chopped fresh cilantro
- 1 tbsp snipped fresh garlic chives
- 1 tbsp balsamic vinegar
- salt and pepper
- fresh garlic chives, to garnish

1 Set aside 3 tablespoons of the chicken stock and bring the remainder to a boil in a large pan. Add the rice and cook for 30 minutes, or until tender. Drain and let cool slightly.

2 Meanwhile, heat 1 tablespoon of the oil in a preheated wok or skillet. Stir-fry the turkey over medium heat for 3–4 minutes, or until cooked through. Using a slotted spoon, transfer the turkey to a dish. Add the snow peas and mushrooms to the wok and stir-fry for 1 minute. Add the reserved stock, bring to a boil, then reduce the heat, cover, and let simmer for 3–4 minutes. Transfer the vegetables to the dish and let cool slightly.

3 Thoroughly mix the rice, turkey, snow peas, mushrooms, nuts, cilantro, and garlic chives together, then season to taste with salt and pepper. Drizzle with the remaining corn oil and the vinegar and garnish with fresh garlic chives. Serve warm.

turkey salad pockets

makes 2

- small handful baby leaf spinach, rinsed, patted dry, and shredded
- ½ red bell pepper, seeded and thinly sliced
- ½ carrot, peeled and coarsely grated
- 4 tbsp hummus
- ⅔ cup bite-size, cooked, skinless, turkey pieces
- ½ tbsp toasted sunflower seeds
- 1 whole wheat pita
- salt and pepper

1 Preheat the broiler to high. Put the spinach leaves, bell pepper, carrot, and hummus into a large bowl and stir together, so all the salad ingredients are coated with the hummus. Stir in the turkey and sunflower seeds and season to taste with salt and pepper.

2 Put the pita under the broiler for about 1 minute on each side to warm through, but do not brown. Cut it in half to make 2 "pockets" of bread.

3 Divide the salad among the bread pockets and serve.

roast duck salad

serves 4
- 2 duck breasts
- 2 Boston lettuce, shredded
- 1 cup bean sprouts
- 1 yellow bell pepper, seeded and cut into thin strips
- ½ cucumber, seeded and cut into short thin sticks
- shredded lime zest and shredded coconut, toasted, to garnish

dressing
- juice of 2 limes
- 3 tbsp Thai fish sauce
- 1 tbsp brown sugar
- 2 tsp sweet chili sauce
- 1-inch/2.5-cm piece fresh ginger, finely grated
- 3 tbsp chopped fresh mint
- 3 tbsp chopped fresh basil

1 Preheat the oven to 400°F/200°C. Place the duck breasts on a rack set over a roasting pan and roast in the oven for 20–30 minutes, or until cooked as desired and the skin is crisp. Remove from the oven and set aside to cool.

2 In a large bowl, combine the lettuce, bean sprouts, bell pepper, and cucumber. Cut the cooled duck into slices and add to the salad. Mix well.

3 To make the dressing, whisk the dressing ingredients together in a separate bowl. Add the dressing to the salad and toss well.

4 Turn the salad out onto a serving platter and garnish with the shredded lime zest and coconut before serving.

warm duck, shallot & orange salad

serves 4

- 2 large oranges
- 4 duck breast fillets, about 6 oz/175 g each
- 12 small shallots, halved
- 1 tbsp sugar
- 2 tbsp olive oil
- 1 tbsp red wine vinegar
- 1¾ cups baby spinach leaves
- 1¾ cups baby red Swiss chard leaves
- salt and pepper

1 Preheat the oven to 400°F/200°C. Halve and squeeze the juice from 1 of the oranges. Using a serrated knife, remove all the peel and white pith from the other orange, then halve and thinly slice.

2 Season the duck fillets with salt and pepper. Heat a large heavy skillet and add the duck fillets, skin-side down. Cook over medium–high heat for 5–6 minutes, until the skin is golden brown. Turn over and cook for another minute. Transfer the duck fillets to a shallow roasting pan and roast in the oven for 10 minutes, or a little longer if you prefer the duck well done.

3 Add the shallots to the skillet and turn to coat in the duck fat. Cook gently for 7–8 minutes, until golden and tender. Remove with a slotted spoon and keep warm. Pour the orange juice into the skillet and bring to a boil. Whisk in the sugar, oil, and vinegar and simmer for 2–3 minutes, until just syrupy. Season to taste with salt and pepper.

4 Put the spinach, Swiss chard leaves, and orange slices onto 4 serving plates. Slice each duck fillet and place on top of the salad with the shallots. Spoon the warm dressing over them and serve immediately.

duck & radish salad

serves 4
- 12 oz/350 g boneless duck breasts
- 2 tbsp all-purpose flour
- 1 egg
- 2 tbsp water
- 2 tbsp sesame seeds
- 3 tbsp sesame oil
- ½ head Chinese cabbage, shredded
- 3 celery stalks, sliced finely
- 8 radishes, trimmed and halved
- salt and pepper
- fresh basil leaves, to garnish

dressing
- finely grated peel of 1 lime
- 2 tbsp lime juice
- 2 tbsp olive oil
- 1 tbsp light soy sauce
- 1 tbsp chopped fresh basil

1 Put each duck breast between sheets of parchment paper or plastic wrap. Use a meat mallet or rolling pin to beat them out and flatten them slightly. Sprinkle the flour onto a large plate and season with salt and pepper. Beat together the egg and water in a shallow bowl, then sprinkle the sesame seeds onto a separate plate.

2 Dip the duck breasts first into the seasoned flour, then into the egg mixture, and finally into the sesame seeds to coat the duck evenly. Heat a wok or large skillet over medium heat and add the sesame oil. When hot, add the duck breasts and fry for about 8 minutes, turning once. To test whether they are cooked, insert a sharp knife into the thickest part—the juices should run clear. Lift them out and drain on paper towels.

3 To make the dressing, whisk the dressing ingredients together in a separate bowl. Arrange the Chinese cabbage, celery, and radishes on a serving plate. Slice the duck breasts thinly and place on top of the salad. Drizzle with the dressing and garnish with fresh basil leaves. Serve at once.

duck salad with sweet chili dressing

serves 4

- 2 duck legs, about 6 oz/175 g each
- 1 tsp five-spice powder
- 2¾ cups sugar snap peas
- 1 small iceberg lettuce, finely shredded
- 2 celery stalks, very thinly sliced
- 6 scallions, finely shredded

dressing

- 1 tbsp sunflower oil
- 3 tbsp sweet chili sauce
- 1 tbsp rice vinegar
- salt and pepper

1 Preheat the oven to 400°F/200°C. Put the duck legs into a roasting pan and pour 1¼ cups boiling water over the skin. Drain off the water and pat the skins dry with paper towels.

2 Rub the five-spice powder into the duck skin. Roast the duck legs in the oven for 1¼–1½ hours, until cooked through with golden crispy skin. Let cool for 10 minutes.

3 To make the dressing, whisk the dressing ingredients together in a separate bowl.

4 Bring a small pan of water to a boil and add the sugar snap peas. Cook for 2 minutes, then drain and refresh under cold running water. Thinly slice the sugar snap peas lengthwise and put them into a bowl with the lettuce, celery, and nearly all the scallions. Toss well to mix.

5 Peel off the crispy skin from the roast duck and cut it into thin strips. Using 2 forks, pull and shred all the duck flesh from the bones.

6 Transfer the salad to a platter and top with the shredded duck and crispy skin. Drizzle the dressing over it and garnish with the rest of the scallions. Serve immediately.

duck & noodle salad with peanut sauce

serves 3
- 2 carrots, peeled
- 2 celery stalks
- 1 cucumber
- 3 duck breasts, about 5 oz/140 g each
- 12 oz/350 g rice noodles, cooked according to the package directions, rinsed, and drained

peanut sauce
- 2 garlic cloves, crushed
- 2 tbsp dark brown sugar
- 2 tbsp peanut butter
- 2 tbsp coconut cream
- 2 tbsp soy sauce
- 2 tbsp rice vinegar
- 2 tbsp sesame oil
- ½ tsp pepper
- ½ tsp Chinese five-spice powder
- ½ tsp ground ginger

1 Preheat the broiler. Cut the carrots, celery, and cucumber into thin strips and set aside.

2 Broil the duck breasts for about 5 minutes on each side, until cooked through. Let cool.

3 Meanwhile, heat all the ingredients for the peanut sauce in a small pan until combined and the sugar has dissolved completely. Stir until smooth.

4 Slice the duck breasts. Divide the noodles among 3 serving bowls. Place the reserved carrots, celery, and cucumber on top of the noodles, arrange the duck slices on top, and drizzle with the sauce. Serve immediately.

duck salad with plum & chile

serves 4

- 6 oz/175 g duck breast, trimmed of any visible fat
- 2–3 sprays sunflower oil
- 1-inch/2.5-cm piece fresh ginger, peeled and grated
- 1 fresh serrano chile, seeded and sliced
- 1 red onion, cut into thin wedges
- 2 celery stalks, trimmed and finely sliced
- 1 small red bell pepper, seeded and finely sliced
- 1 tbsp soy sauce
- 1 cup sliced zucchini
- 2 ripe but still firm plums, pitted and sliced
- 1 cup shredded bok choy
- 1 tbsp chopped fresh cilantro

1 Cut the duck breast into thin strips and set aside. Heat a wok until very hot, then spray with the oil and heat for 30 seconds. Add the ginger, chile, and duck strips and stir-fry for 1–2 minutes, or until the duck strips are browned.

2 Add the onion wedges, celery, and red bell pepper slices and continue to stir-fry for 3 minutes.

3 Add the soy sauce, zucchini, and plums to the wok and stir-fry for 2 minutes before stirring in the shredded bok choy and the chopped cilantro. Stir-fry for an additional minute, then serve, divided equally among 4 bowls.

Mmmm...
fish &
seafood

niçoise pasta salad

serves 4
- 12 oz/350 g dried conchiglie (pasta shells)
- 4 oz/115 g green beans
- 1¾ oz/50 g canned anchovy fillets, drained
- 2 tbsp milk
- 2 small heads of crisp lettuce
- 3 large tomatoes
- 4 hard-cooked eggs
- 8 oz/225 g canned tuna, drained
- 1 cup pitted black olives
- salt

vinaigrette
- ¼ cup extra virgin olive oil
- 2 tbsp white wine vinegar
- 1 tsp whole-grain mustard
- salt and pepper

1 Bring a large pan of lightly salted water to a boil over medium heat. Add the pasta and cook for 8–10 minutes, or according to the package directions, until tender but still firm to the bite. Drain the pasta thoroughly and refresh in cold water.

2 Bring a small pan of lightly salted water to a boil over medium heat. Add the beans and cook for 5 minutes, or until done. Drain thoroughly and refresh in cold water, then drain again and set aside.

3 Put the anchovies into a shallow bowl, then pour over the milk and set aside for 10 minutes. Meanwhile, tear the lettuce into large pieces. Blanch the tomatoes in boiling water for 1–2 minutes, then drain. Skin and coarsely chop the flesh. Shell the eggs and cut into quarters. Flake the tuna into large chunks.

4 Drain the anchovies and the pasta. Put all the salad ingredients into a large bowl and gently mix together.

5 To make the vinaigrette, beat the oil, vinegar, and mustard together, season to taste with salt and pepper, and keep in the refrigerator until ready to serve. Just before serving, pour the vinaigrette over the salad.

caramelized tuna salad

serves 4

- scant 1 cup fresh bean sprouts
- 4-inch/10-cm piece of cucumber
- 1½ cups cilantro leaves
- 1½ cups mint leaves
- 1 tsp sesame oil, plus a few drops for drizzling
- 1 tbsp peanut oil
- 1 lb/450 g fresh tuna, cut into 1-inch/2.5-cm chunks
- salt
- 2 tbsp salted roasted peanuts, crushed, to garnish

dressing

- 2 tsp canola oil
- 1 tsp finely chopped fresh ginger
- ½–1 small fresh red chile, seeded and finely chopped
- 4 tbsp light soy sauce
- 1 tbsp Thai fish sauce
- 1 tbsp tamarind paste
- ⅓ cup brown sugar

1 To make the dressing, heat a small wok over high heat. Add the oil and fry the ginger and chile for a few seconds. Add the soy sauce, Thai fish sauce, and tamarind paste. Stir for 30 seconds, then add the sugar and stir until dissolved. Remove the wok from the heat and set aside.

2 Rinse the bean sprouts in boiling water and drain. Blot dry with paper towels. Peel the cucumber, halve lengthwise, and scoop out the seeds. Thinly slice the flesh diagonally.

3 Put the bean sprouts, cucumber, cilantro, and mint leaves in a bowl. Season with a pinch of salt and a few drops of sesame oil. Toss to combine, then divide among individual serving plates.

4 Heat a large wok over a high heat, then add the sesame and peanut oils. Quickly stir-fry the tuna, turning with tongs, until colored on the outside but still slightly red in the middle. Arrange the tuna chunks on top of the salad.

5 Reheat the dressing, thinning with a spoonful of water if necessary, and pour over the tuna. Sprinkle with the crushed peanuts and serve at once.

tuna, lentil & potato salad

serves 4

- 1 cup French green or brown lentils
- 2 tbsp olive oil, plus extra for brushing
- 10½ oz/300 g baby new potatoes, washed
- 1 head Boston lettuce
- 4 fresh tuna steaks, about 3½ oz/100 g each
- 12 small cherry tomatoes, halved
- 2 cups arugula leaves

dressing

- 5 tbsp fruity olive oil
- 1 tbsp balsamic vinegar
- 2 tsp red wine vinegar
- 1 tsp smooth Dijon mustard
- 1 tsp light brown sugar

1 Cook the lentils in a saucepan of boiling water for 25 minutes, or until tender. Drain, then turn into a bowl and stir in the oil.

2 Meanwhile, cook the potatoes in a separate saucepan of lightly salted water for 15 minutes, or until just tender.

3 Break off the outer lettuce leaves and cut the heart into 8 even pieces. Arrange on 4 individual serving plates.

4 To make the dressing, place all the ingredients in a screw-top jar and shake vigorously until they are well blended.

5 When the potatoes are nearly cooked, lightly brush a ridged grill pan with oil and heat over high heat. When very hot, add the tuna steaks and cook for 1½ minutes on each side to sear. Remove to a cutting board and cut each steak into 6 chunks.

6 Drain the potatoes and coarsely chop any larger ones. Arrange with the lentils, tuna, and tomatoes on the serving plates, then sprinkle over the arugula leaves and spoon over the dressing. Serve immediately.

tuna & two-bean salad

serves 4
- 7 oz/200 g green beans
- 14 oz/400 g canned small white beans, such as cannellini, rinsed and drained
- 4 scallions, finely chopped
- 2 fresh tuna steaks, about 8 oz/225 g each and ¾ inch/2 cm thick
- olive oil, for brushing
- 1⅔ cups halved cherry tomatoes
- handful lettuce leaves
- salt and pepper
- fresh mint and flat-leaf parsley sprigs, to garnish

dressing
- handful fresh mint leaves, shredded
- handful fresh flat-leaf parsley leaves, chopped
- 1 garlic clove, crushed
- 4 tbsp extra virgin olive oil
- 1 tbsp red wine vinegar
- salt and pepper

1 To make the dressing, place all the ingredients in a screw-top jar and shake vigorously until they are well blended.

2 Bring a pan of lightly salted water to a boil. Add the green beans and cook for 3 minutes. Add the white beans and cook for another 4 minutes, until the green beans are tender-crisp and the white beans are heated through. Drain well and add to the bowl with the dressing and scallions. Toss together.

3 To cook the tuna, heat a stove-top ridged grill pan over high heat. Lightly brush the tuna steaks with oil, then season to taste with salt and pepper. Cook the steaks for 2 minutes, then turn over and cook on the other side for another 2 minutes for rare or up to 4 minutes for well done.

4 Remove the tuna from the grill pan and let rest for 2 minutes, or alternatively let stand until completely cool. When ready to serve, add the tomatoes to the bean mixture and toss lightly. Line a serving platter with the lettuce leaves and pile on the bean salad. Place the tuna over the top. Serve warm or at room temperature, garnished with the herbs.

smoked salmon & arugula salad

serves 4

- 2½ cups wild arugula leaves
- 1 tbsp chopped fresh flat-leaf parsley, plus extra sprigs, to garnish
- 2 scallions, finely diced
- 2 large avocados
- 1 tbsp lemon juice
- 9 oz/250 g smoked salmon

dressing

- ⅔ cup mayonnaise
- 2 tbsp lime juice
- finely grated rind of 1 lime
- 1 tbsp chopped fresh flat-leaf parsley

1 Shred the arugula and arrange in 4 individual bowls. Sprinkle over the chopped parsley and scallions.

2 Halve, peel, and pit the avocados and cut into thin slices or small chunks. Brush with the lemon juice to prevent discoloration, then divide among the salad bowls. Mix together gently. Cut the smoked salmon into strips and sprinkle over the top.

3 To make the dressing, whisk the dressing ingredients together in a separate bowl. Spoon some of the dressing on top of each salad and garnish with parsley sprigs.

teriyaki salmon salad

serves 4

- 6 scallions, finely shredded
- 4 salmon fillets (with skin), about 4 oz/115 g each
- 4 tbsp teriyaki sauce
- 8 oz/225 g cellophane noodles
- 2 tsp toasted sesame oil
- 1 tsp grated fresh ginger
- 1 green bell pepper, seeded and finely shredded
- 2 carrots, finely shredded
- 2 tbsp sesame seeds
- 2 tbsp rice vinegar
- salt and pepper
- lime wedges, to serve

1 Put half of the shredded scallions into a small bowl of cold water with a couple of ice cubes. Let stand in the refrigerator for at least 1 hour, until the scallions are curly. Put the salmon fillets into a shallow dish and pour the teriyaki sauce over them. Cover and let marinate at room temperature for 30 minutes.

2 Cook the noodles in a large pan of lightly salted boiling water for 3 minutes, or according to the package directions, until just tender. Drain well and refresh under cold running water. Transfer to a bowl. Heat the oil in a wok and add the ginger, bell pepper, carrots, and remaining scallions. Stir-fry for 1 minute. Add the sesame seeds and stir-fry for an additional minute. Cool for 10 minutes, then add to the noodles with the vinegar, and toss well to mix. Season with salt and pepper.

3 Heat a nonstick skillet and add the salmon fillets, skin-side down. Cook for 1 minute on each side, until browned. Pour in the teriyaki marinade. Reduce the heat and cook for another 3–4 minutes on each side, until just cooked through. Divide the noodle salad among 4 serving plates and top each with a salmon fillet. Drain the scallion curls and pat dry with paper towels. Put them on top of the salmon fillets and serve with lime wedges.

warm salmon & mango salad

serves 4

- 8 red or yellow cherry tomatoes
- 3 oz/85 g salmon fillets, skinned and cut into small cubes
- 1 large ripe mango, cut into small chunks (about ¾ cup)
- 2 tbsp orange juice
- 1 tbsp soy sauce
- 4 cups assorted salad greens
- ½ cucumber, trimmed and sliced into thin sticks
- 6 scallions, trimmed and chopped

dressing

- 4 tbsp low-fat plain yogurt
- 1 tsp soy sauce
- 1 tbsp finely grated orange rind

1 Soak 4 kebab sticks in cold water for 30 minutes, then drain. Cut half the tomatoes in half and set aside. Thread the salmon with the whole tomatoes and half the mango chunks onto the 4 kebab sticks. Mix the orange juice and soy sauce together in a small bowl and brush over the kebabs. Let marinate for 15 minutes, brushing with the remaining orange juice mixture at least once more.

2 Arrange the salad greens on a serving platter with the reserved halved tomatoes, mango chunks, the cucumber sticks, and scallions. Preheat the broiler to high and line the broiler rack with foil. To make the dressing, whisk the dressing ingredients together in a separate bowl.

3 Place the salmon kebabs on the broiler rack, brush again with the marinade, and broil for 5-7 minutes, or until the salmon is cooked. Turn the kebabs over halfway through cooking and brush with any remaining marinade.

4 Divide the prepared salad among 4 plates, top each with a kebab, and then drizzle with the dressing.

tomato, salmon & shrimp salad

serves 4
- 8 cherry or baby plum tomatoes
- handful lettuce leaves
- 4 ripe tomatoes, coarsely chopped
- 3½ oz/100 g smoked salmon
- 7 oz/200 g large cooked shrimp, thawed if frozen
- pepper

dressing
- 1 tbsp Dijon mustard
- 2 tsp superfine sugar
- 2 tsp red wine vinegar
- 2 tbsp medium olive oil
- few fresh dill sprigs, plus extra to garnish

1 Halve most of the cherry tomatoes. Place the lettuce leaves around the edge of a shallow bowl and add all of the tomatoes and cherry tomatoes. Using scissors, snip the smoked salmon into strips and sprinkle over the tomatoes, then add the shrimp.

2 To make the dressing, mix the mustard, sugar, vinegar, and oil together in a small bowl, then tear most of the dill sprigs into it. Mix well and pour over the salad. Toss well to coat the salad with the dressing. Before serving, snip the remaining dill over the top and season to taste with pepper.

salt cod salad

Serves 4–6

- 14 oz/400 g dried salt cod in one piece
- 6 scallions, sliced thinly on the diagonal
- 6 tbsp extra virgin olive oil
- 1 tbsp sherry vinegar
- 1 tbsp lemon juice
- 2 large red bell peppers, broiled, peeled, seeded, and diced very finely
- 12 large black olives, pitted and sliced
- 2 large, juicy tomatoes, sliced thinly, to serve
- 2 tbsp very finely chopped fresh parsley, to garnish
- salt and pepper

1 Place the dried salt cod in a large bowl, cover with cold water, and let soak for at least 48 hours, changing the water occasionally.

2 Pat the salt cod dry with paper towels and remove the skin and bones, then use your fingers to tear into fine shreds. Put in a large, nonmetallic bowl with the scallions, oil, vinegar, and lemon juice, and toss together. Season with pepper, cover, and put in the refrigerator to marinate for 3 hours.

3 Stir in the bell peppers and olives. Taste and adjust the seasoning, if necessary, remembering that the cod and olives might be salty. Arrange the tomato slices on a large platter or individual plates and spoon the salad on top. Sprinkle with parsley and serve.

smoked trout & pear salad

serves 4
- 2 ripe red Bartlett pears,
- 1 tbsp lemon juice
- 3 heads Belgian endive, trimmed and leaves separated
- ½ bunch watercress, coarse stalks removed
- 8 oz/225 g smoked trout fillets
- ½ cup green grapes, halved

dressing
- 4 tbsp sour cream
- 1 tbsp milk
- 1 tsp creamed horseradish
- 2 tsp lemon juice
- salt and pepper

1 Core and slice the pears then toss with the lemon juice to prevent discoloration. Put them into a serving dish with the endive leaves and watercress.

2 Flake the smoked trout, removing any skin and fine bones. Sprinkle it over the salad with the grapes.

3 To make the dressing, whisk the dressing ingredients together in a separate bowl. Drizzle the dressing over the salad just before serving. Season with a little more pepper.

sweet & sour fish salad

serves 4
- 8 oz/225 g trout fillets
- 8 oz/225 g white fish fillets (such as cod)
- 1¼ cups water
- 1 stem lemongrass
- 2 lime leaves
- 1 large red chile
- 1 bunch scallions, trimmed and shredded
- 1 cup diced fresh pineapple
- 1 small red bell pepper, seeded and diced
- 1 bunch watercress, washed and trimmed
- fresh snipped chives, to garnish

dressing
- 1 tbsp sunflower oil
- 1 tbsp rice wine vinegar
- pinch of chili powder
- 1 tsp honey
- salt and pepper

1 Rinse the fish, place in a skillet, and pour over the water. Bend the lemongrass in half to bruise it and add to the skillet with the lime leaves. Prick the chile with a fork and add to the pan. Bring to a boil and simmer for 7–8 minutes. Let cool.

2 Drain the fish fillets thoroughly, then flake the flesh away from the skin and place it in a bowl. Gently stir in the scallions, pineapple, and bell pepper.

3 Arrange the washed watercress on 4 serving plates and spoon the cooked fish mixture on top.

4 To make the dressing, mix the dressing ingredients together in a separate bowl. Spoon it over the fish and serve the salad garnished with chives.

spiced fish skewers & tomato salad

serves 4

- 1 lb/450 g cod loin or monkfish, cut into 1-inch/2.5-cm cubes
- 3 tbsp lime juice
- 4 tbsp sunflower oil
- 2 tsp mild chili powder
- 1 tsp dried oregano
- 1 lemon, cut into 8 wedges
- 16 red cherry tomatoes, halved
- 16 yellow cherry tomatoes, halved
- ½ small onion, thinly sliced
- 2 tbsp coarsely chopped fresh cilantro
- ½ tsp sugar
- 1 tsp mild mustard
- salt and pepper

1 Put the fish cubes into a shallow bowl. Combine 2 tablespoons of the lime juice and 2 tablespoons of the oil with the chili powder and oregano in a pitcher. Season with salt and pepper and pour the mixture over the fish. Cover and let marinate at room temperature for 1 hour.

2 Preheat the broiler to medium. Thread the pieces of fish and two lemon wedges onto each metal skewer and cook the skewers, turning occasionally, for 8–10 minutes, until just cooked.

3 Meanwhile, combine the tomatoes, onion, and cilantro in a bowl. Whisk the remaining lime juice and oil together with the sugar and mustard. Pour the dressing over the tomatoes and toss well to mix. Season with salt and pepper.

4 Divide the tomato salad among 4 serving dishes and top each with 2 fish skewers. Serve immediately.

seared swordfish with salsa

serves 4

- 4 boneless swordfish steaks, about 5 oz/140 g each
- ½ cup (1 stick) butter
- 1 tbsp olive oil
- salt
- fresh crusty bread, to serve

tomato & olive salsa

- 4 tbsp extra virgin olive oil
- 1 tbsp red wine vinegar
- 1 lb 5 oz/600 g ripe, juicy beef tomatoes, cored, seeded, and finely chopped
- ¾ cup large black olives, pitted and cut in half
- 1 shallot, finely chopped or thinly sliced
- 1 tbsp capers in brine, rinsed and dried
- 3 tbsp finely shredded fresh basil leaves
- salt and pepper

1 To make the tomato & olive salsa, whisk the olive oil and vinegar together in a bowl large enough to hold all the ingredients. Gently stir in the tomatoes, olives, shallot, and capers with salt and pepper to taste. Cover and chill until required.

2 Season the swordfish steaks on both sides with salt. Melt the butter with the oil in a skillet large enough to hold the swordfish steaks in a single layer. (If you don't have a large enough pan, cook the steaks in 2 batches.)

3 Add the swordfish steaks to the pan in a single layer and fry for about 3 minutes, until golden brown, then carefully turn the fish over and continue frying for an additional 3 minutes, until the fish is cooked through and flakes easily. Remove the fish from the pan and set aside to cool completely. Cover and chill for at least 2 hours.

4 When ready to serve, remove the fish from the refrigerator at least 15 minutes in advance. Stir the basil into the salsa, then adjust the seasoning if necessary. Break the swordfish into large flakes and gently stir into the salsa—be careful to avoid breaking up the fish too much. Arrange the fish salad in 4 bowls, spooning over any of the leftover juices, and serve with crusty bread.

warm mackerel
& potato salad

serves 4
- 4 mackerel fillets, about 5 oz/140 g each
- 1 tsp coarsely ground black pepper
- thinly pared rind and juice of 1 small lemon
- 1 tbsp extra virgin olive oil
- 1 lb/450 g new potatoes, sliced
- 4 scallions, thinly sliced
- 1¼ cups wild arugula leaves
- fresh dill sprigs, to garnish

dressing
- 5 tbsp extra virgin olive oil
- 2 tbsp white wine vinegar
- 1 tsp Dijon mustard
- pinch of sugar
- 1 tbsp chopped fresh dill
- salt and pepper

1 Make 3–4 diagonal slashes in the skin of each mackerel fillet and put them into a dish. Combine the coarsely ground pepper, lemon rind and juice, and oil and pour the mixture over the fillets. Cover and let marinate at room temperature for 20 minutes.

2 Preheat the broiler. Cook the mackerel fillets under the broiler, turning once, for 7–8 minutes, until just cooked through. Meanwhile, cook the potatoes in a pan of lightly salted boiling water for 10–12 minutes, until tender. To make the dressing, whisk the dressing ingredients together in a separate bowl.

3 Drain the potatoes and mix gently with the scallions and half the dressing. Divide among 4 serving plates and add the arugula leaves. Top each salad with a hot mackerel fillet and drizzle the rest of the dressing over them. Garnish with fresh dill sprigs and serve.

anchovy & olive salad

serves 4
- handful mixed lettuce leaves
- 12 cherry tomatoes, halved
- 20 black olives, pitted and halved
- 6 canned anchovy fillets, drained and sliced
- 1 tbsp chopped fresh oregano
- wedges of lemon, to garnish
- fresh crusty bread rolls, to serve

dressing
- 4 tbsp extra virgin olive oil
- 1 tbsp white wine vinegar
- 1 tbsp lemon juice
- 1 tbsp chopped fresh flat-leaf parsley
- salt and pepper

1 To make the dressing, stir the dressing ingredients together in a bowl.

2 To assemble the salad, arrange the lettuce leaves in a serving dish. Scatter the cherry tomatoes on top, followed by the olives, anchovies, and oregano. Drizzle over the dressing.

3 Transfer to individual plates, garnish with lemon wedges, and serve with crusty bread rolls.

shrimp & white bean salad

serves 4

- 14 oz/400 g canned cannellini beans, drained and rinsed
- ½ red onion, finely chopped
- 1 celery stalk, finely diced
- 10½ oz/300 g cooked, large, peeled shrimp with tails intact
- 1 garlic clove, finely chopped
- juice of 1 lemon
- 5 tbsp extra virgin olive oil
- handful of fresh flat-leaf parsley leaves, plus 2 tbsp chopped
- 4 thick slices rustic bread
- 6 baby plum tomatoes, halved
- salt and pepper

1 Put the beans, onion, celery, shrimp, and garlic into a large shallow bowl. Add the lemon juice, 2 tablespoons of the oil, and the chopped parsley. Season lightly with salt and pepper. Stir well, then cover and set aside.

2 Brush the slices of bread with some of the remaining olive oil. Cook on a hot stove-top grill pan for 2–3 minutes on each side, until golden, or toast under a hot broiler. Put them on 4 serving plates.

3 Gently stir the tomatoes and the handful of parsley leaves into the salad. Pile the salad onto the hot toasts. Drizzle the rest of the olive oil over the salad, season with a little more pepper, and serve.

shrimp & rice salad

serves 4

- scant 1 cup mixed long-grain and wild rice
- 12 oz/350 g cooked peeled shrimp
- 1 mango, peeled, pitted, and diced
- 4 scallions, sliced
- ¼ cup slivered almonds
- 1 tbsp finely chopped fresh mint
- salt and pepper

dressing

- 1 tbsp extra virgin olive oil
- 2 tsp lime juice
- 1 garlic clove, crushed
- 1 tsp honey
- salt and pepper

1 Cook the rice in a large pan of lightly salted boiling water for 35 minutes, or until tender. Drain and transfer to a large bowl, then add the shrimp.

2 To make the dressing, mix all the ingredients together in a measuring pitcher, seasoning to taste with the salt and pepper, and whisk well until thoroughly blended. Pour the dressing over the rice-and-shrimp mixture and let cool.

3 Add the mango, scallions, almonds, and mint to the salad and season to taste with pepper. Stir thoroughly, transfer to a large serving dish, and serve.

coconut shrimp salad

serves 4

- 1 cup brown basmati rice
- ½ tsp coriander seeds
- 2 egg whites, lightly beaten
- generous ¾ cup dry unsweetened coconut
- 24 jumbo shrimp, peeled and deveined
- ½ cucumber
- 4 scallions, thinly sliced lengthwise
- 1 tsp sesame oil
- 1 tbsp finely chopped fresh cilantro

1 Bring a large pan of water to a boil, add the rice, and cook for 25 minutes, or until tender. Drain and keep in a strainer covered with a clean dish towel to absorb the steam. Meanwhile, soak 8 wooden skewers in cold water for 30 minutes, then drain. Crush the coriander seeds in a mortar with a pestle. Heat a nonstick skillet over medium heat, add the crushed coriander seeds, and cook, turning, until they start to color. Turn onto a plate and set aside.

2 Put the egg whites into a shallow bowl and the coconut into a separate bowl. Roll each shrimp first in the egg whites, then in the coconut. Thread onto a skewer. Repeat so that each skewer is threaded with 3 coated shrimp. Preheat the broiler to high. Using a vegetable peeler, peel long strips from the cucumber to create ribbons, put into a strainer to drain, then toss with the scallions and oil in a bowl and set aside.

3 Cook the shrimp under the preheated broiler for 3–4 minutes on each side, or until slightly browned. Meanwhile, mix the rice with the toasted coriander seeds and fresh cilantro and divide this and the cucumber salad among the bowls. Serve with the hot shrimp skewers.

thai crab patty salad

serves 4

- 12 oz/350 g canned white crabmeat, drained
- 5 oz/140 g cooked, peeled shrimp
- 1 tsp lime juice
- 2 tsp Thai red curry paste
- 1 tbsp beaten egg white
- 1 tbsp chopped fresh cilantro, plus 2 tbsp chopped fresh cilantro stalks
- 1 tbsp all-purpose flour, plus extra for dusting
- sunflower oil, for shallow-frying
- ½ cucumber, peeled, seeded, and thinly sliced
- 4 cups bean sprouts
- ½ cup cress
- 1 tbsp rice vinegar
- 4 tbsp sweet chili sauce
- salt and pepper
- lime wedges, to garnish

1 Put the crab, shrimp, lime juice, and curry paste into a food processor and process for a few seconds until finely ground. Add the egg white and chopped cilantro leaves and season well with salt and pepper. Process for a few seconds more until well mixed.

2 Transfer the mixture to a bowl and, using lightly floured hands, shape into 12 small patties. Coat lightly in the flour. Cover and chill in the refrigerator for 1 hour.

3 Heat the oil in a large skillet and fry the crab patties, in 2 batches, turning once, for 3–4 minutes, until golden brown. Drain on paper towels.

4 Put the cucumber, bean sprouts, cress, and cilantro stalks into a bowl and toss with the rice vinegar. Divide among 4 serving plates. Top with the hot crab patties and spoon the chili sauce over them. Serve garnished with lime wedges.

spicy warm crab salad

serves 4

- 2 sprays sunflower oil
- 1 fresh serrano chile, seeded and finely chopped
- generous 1 cup diagonally halved snow peas
- 6 scallions, trimmed and finely shredded
- 2 heaping tbsp frozen corn kernels, defrosted
- 5½ oz/150 g white crabmeat, drained if canned
- 2 oz/55 g shrimp, peeled and deveined, thawed if frozen
- 1 large carrot, peeled and grated
- ¾ cup bean sprouts
- 8 cups baby spinach leaves
- 1 tbsp finely grated orange rind
- 2 tbsp orange juice
- chopped fresh cilantro, to garnish

1 Heat a wok and, when hot, spray in the oil and heat for 30 seconds. Add the chile and snow peas, then stir-fry over medium heat for 2 minutes.

2 Add the scallions and corn and continue to stir-fry for an additional 1 minute.

3 Add the crabmeat, shrimp, carrot, bean sprouts, and spinach leaves. Stir in the orange rind and juice and stir-fry for 2–3 minutes, or until the spinach has begun to wilt and everything is cooked. Serve divided equally among 4 bowls, sprinkled with the chopped cilantro.

lobster & summer herb salad

serves 4–6

- 1 lb 10 oz–1 lb 12 oz/ 750–800 g freshly cooked lobster meat, cut into bite-size chunks
- 1 large avocado, peeled, pitted, and cut into chunky dice
- 4 ripe but firm tomatoes
- 8 cups mixed herb salad greens, about 9 oz/250 g
- 1–2 tbsp fruity olive oil
- squeeze of lemon juice
- salt and pepper

saffron mayonnaise

- pinch of saffron threads
- 1 egg
- 1 tsp Dijon mustard
- 1 tbsp white wine vinegar
- pinch of salt
- 1¼ cups sunflower oil
- salt and pepper

1 For the mayonnaise, soak the saffron threads in a little warm water. Meanwhile, put the egg, mustard, vinegar, and salt in a food processor or blender and process to combine. With the motor running, slowly trickle in about one-third of the sunflower oil. Once the mixture starts to thicken, add the remaining oil more quickly. When all the oil has been incorporated, add the saffron and its soaking water and process to combine. Add more salt and pepper to taste, then cover and refrigerate until required.

2 Put the lobster meat and avocado in a bowl. Quarter the tomatoes and remove the seeds. Cut the flesh into fairly chunky dice and add to the bowl. Season the lobster mixture to taste with salt and pepper and gently stir in enough of the mayonnaise to give everything a light coating. Toss the salad greens with the olive oil and lemon juice. Divide among plates and top with the lobster mixture. Serve immediately.

layered crayfish salad

serves 4

- generous ¾ cup grated carrots
- 1 Boston lettuce, shredded
- ¼ cucumber, diced
- ½ cup drained, canned corn kernels
- 6 oz/175 g cooked crayfish tails in brine, thoroughly drained
- ½ tsp cayenne pepper
- lemon wedges, to garnish (optional)

dressing

- ½ cup mayonnaise
- 1 tbsp ketchup
- dash of Worcestershire sauce
- 1 tbsp lemon juice
- salt and pepper

1 To make the dressing, mix the dressing ingredients together in a bowl.

2 Divide the grated carrot among 4 individual bowls. Put the shredded lettuce in a layer on top of the carrots, followed by the cucumber and corn.

3 Spoon the dressing over the salad and pile the crayfish tails on top. Sprinkle with the cayenne pepper. Garnish with lemon wedges, if using, and serve.

squid, watercress & baby spinach salad

serves 4
- 12 squid tubes and tentacles, weighing about 1 lb 9 oz/700 g, cleaned and prepared
- 2–3 tbsp olive oil
- 1–2 red chiles, seeded and thinly sliced
- 2 scallions, finely chopped
- lemon wedges, for squeezing and for serving
- 3 good handfuls watercress
- 2 handfuls baby spinach or arugula
- salt and pepper

dressing
- scant ½ cup olive oil
- juice of 1 lime
- 1 tsp superfine sugar
- 2 shallots, thinly sliced
- 1 tomato, peeled, seeded, and finely chopped
- 1 garlic clove, crushed
- salt and pepper

1 To make the dressing, mix all the ingredients together in a bowl, season with salt and pepper to taste, then cover and refrigerate until required.

2 Cut the squid tubes into 2-inch/5-cm pieces, then score diamond patterns lightly across the flesh with the tip of a sharp knife. Heat the oil in a wok or large skillet over high heat, then add the squid pieces and tentacles and stir-fry for 1 minute. Add the chiles and scallions and stir-fry for an additional minute. Season to taste with salt and pepper and add a good squeeze of lemon juice.

3 Mix the watercress and spinach together, then toss with enough of the dressing to coat lightly. Serve immediately with the squid, together with lemon wedges to squeeze over the squid.

mixed seafood salad

serves 4–6

- 2 garlic cloves, crushed
- juice of 1½ lemons
- 4 tbsp extra virgin olive oil
- 2 tbsp chopped fresh flat-leaf parsley
- 1 lb 5 oz/600 g cooked seafood cocktail (shrimp, mussels, clams, calamari rings, cockles)
- 1 oil-cured roasted red bell pepper, sliced into thin strips
- 12 black olives, pitted
- 2 tbsp shredded fresh basil
- salt and pepper

1 Whisk the garlic, lemon juice, oil, and parsley with salt and pepper to taste.

2 Drain the seafood, if necessary, and place in a serving dish. Add the bell pepper strips and olives, then mix with the garlic mixture, turning to coat. Let stand in a cool place for 30 minutes to let the flavors develop.

3 Stir again before serving, check the seasoning, and sprinkle with the basil.

Mmmm...
vegetables & legumes

goat cheese toast & spinach salad

serves 2
- 6 thin slices French bread
- 1 tbsp olive oil
- 4 oz/115 g round goat cheese (with rind), cut into 6 slices
- 3 cups baby spinach leaves
- ½ cup drained sun-dried tomatoes
- pepper
- crusty bread, to serve

dressing
- 3 tbsp extra virgin olive oil
- 1 tbsp sherry vinegar
- 1 tsp whole-grain mustard
- pinch of sugar
- salt and pepper

1 Preheat the broiler to medium. To make the dressing, place all the ingredients in a screw-top jar and shake vigorously until they are well blended.

2 Lightly brush the slices of French bread with olive oil. Toast the slices under the broiler for 1–2 minutes on each side, until just golden. Top each with a slice of goat cheese, season with pepper, and broil for another 1–2 minutes, until the cheese has melted.

3 Meanwhile, put the spinach into a large bowl. Add nearly all the dressing and toss gently to coat the leaves. Divide between 2 serving plates. Add the sun-dried tomatoes and top with the cheese toast. Drizzle with the rest of the dressing and serve immediately with crusty bread.

lentil & goat cheese salad

serves 1

- 2 tbsp French green or brown lentils
- 1 bay leaf
- 2 scallions, finely chopped
- scant ¼ cup diced red bell pepper
- 1 tbsp chopped fresh parsley
- 6 cherry tomatoes, halved
- ⅓ cup arugula
- 1 oz/25 g goat cheese, sliced or crumbled

dressing

- 1 tsp olive oil
- 1 tsp balsamic vinegar
- ½ tsp honey
- 1 garlic clove, crushed or finely chopped

1 Rinse the lentils and put in a medium-size pan. Add the bay leaf and cover with plenty of cold water. Bring to a boil, then reduce the heat, and simmer for 20–30 minutes, or until the lentils are tender.

2 Drain the lentils, remove and discard the bay leaf, and transfer the lentils to a bowl. Add the scallions, bell pepper, parsley, cherry tomatoes, and arugula. Mix well.

3 To make the dressing, whisk together the oil, vinegar, honey, and garlic. Serve the salad sprinkled with goat cheese and the dressing.

bean salad with feta

serves 4

- 12 oz/350 g green beans, trimmed
- 1 red onion, chopped
- 3–4 tbsp chopped fresh cilantro
- 2 radishes, thinly sliced
- ¾ cup crumbled feta cheese
- 1 tsp chopped fresh oregano or ½ tsp dried oregano
- 2 tbsp red wine vinegar or fruit vinegar
- 5 tbsp extra virgin olive oil
- 3 ripe tomatoes (optional), cut into wedges
- pepper

1 Bring about 2 inches/5 cm of water to a boil in the bottom of a steamer or in a medium saucepan. Add the green beans to the top of the steamer or place them in a metal colander set over the saucepan of water. Cover and steam the beans for about 5 minutes, until just tender.

2 Transfer the beans to a bowl and add the onion, cilantro, radishes, crumbled feta cheese, and oregano.

3 Grind pepper over to taste. Whisk the vinegar and olive oil together and then pour over the salad. Toss gently to mix well.

4 Transfer to a serving platter, surround with the tomato wedges, if using, and serve at once or chill until ready to serve.

greek feta salad

serves 4
- a few grape leaves
- 4 tomatoes, sliced
- ½ cucumber, peeled and sliced
- 1 small red onion, sliced thinly
- 4 oz/115 g feta cheese, cubed
- 8 black olives
- salt and pepper

dressing
- 3 tbsp extra virgin olive oil
- 1 tbsp lemon juice
- ½ tsp dried oregano

1 To make the dressing, place all the ingredients in a screw-top jar, season to taste with salt and pepper, and shake vigorously until they are well blended.

2 Arrange the grape leaves on a serving dish and then the tomatoes, cucumber, and onion. Sprinkle the cheese and olives on top. Pour the dressing over the salad, season to taste with salt and pepper, and serve.

strawberry & watercress salad

serves 4
- 1 bunch watercress, tough stalks removed
- scant 2½ cups sliced strawberries
- 1 ripe avocado
- 1 tbsp lemon juice
- ¼ cucumber, finely diced
- 1 tbsp chopped walnuts
- salt and pepper

balsamic glaze
- 1 tbsp balsamic vinegar
- 1 tbsp sugar

1 To make the glaze, put the vinegar and sugar into a small pan. Heat gently, stirring, until the sugar dissolves. Simmer gently for 5–6 minutes, until syrupy. Let cool for 30 minutes.

2 Put the watercress into a serving dish. Sprinkle with the strawberries. Halve, pit, peel, and slice the avocado and toss gently in the lemon juice. Add to the salad. Sprinkle with the cucumber and walnuts.

3 Drizzle the glaze over the salad. Season lightly with salt and pepper and serve immediately.

feta, mint, & strawberry salad

serves 4–6

- 1 lb 2 oz/500 g fine green beans
- 1 lb 2 oz/500 g strawberries
- 2–3 tbsp pistachios
- 1 small bunch fresh mint leaves
- 1 lb 2 oz/500 g feta cheese, drained
- pepper

dressing

- 2 tbsp raspberry vinegar
- 2 tsp superfine sugar
- 1 tbsp Dijon mustard
- pinch of salt
- ½ cup olive oil

1 To make the dressing, mix the vinegar, sugar, mustard, and salt together in a bowl until smooth. Slowly pour in the oil, whisking constantly until the mixture has emulsified. Cover and refrigerate until required.

2 Blanch the beans in a large saucepan of salted boiling water for 1–2 minutes, so that they retain plenty of crunch. Drain and quickly toss in a large, cool bowl. Hull and halve the strawberries, then add to the beans. Stir in the pistachios and mint leaves. Toss the salad with enough of the dressing to coat lightly.

3 Break the feta cheese into chunks and scatter over the salad. Add a good grinding of pepper and serve immediately.

pear, arugula & blue cheese salad

serves 4–6

- 1 pear, such as Bosc
- 2 bunches wild arugula, rinsed and shaken dry
- ¾ cup crumbled blue cheese, such as Gorgonzola
- 3 tbsp pine nuts, toasted

dressing

- 4 tbsp extra virgin olive oil
- 1 tbsp balsamic vinegar
- salt and pepper

1 To make the dressing, put the oil, vinegar, and salt and pepper to taste in a large nonmetallic bowl and whisk until blended and thick. Cover and set aside.

2 Just before serving, quarter, core, and thinly slice the pear, adding it to the bowl with the dressing as it is prepared, then gently toss so all the pieces are coated with dressing. Add the arugula and cheese and toss again to combine. Sprinkle the pine nuts over and serve.

melon & grape with mixed salad greens

serves 4

- ½ cup cottage cheese
- 1 tsp chopped fresh parsley
- 1 tbsp snipped fresh chives
- 1 tsp chopped fresh chervil or basil
- 2 assorted colored bell peppers, seeded and peeled
- 1 small melon, such as honeydew or canteloupe
- 6 cups mixed salad greens
- ⅓ cup seedless grapes
- 1 red onion, thinly sliced

dressing

- 3 tbsp freshly squeezed lime juice
- 1 small fresh red chile, seeded and finely chopped
- 1 tsp honey
- 1 tbsp soy sauce

1 Place the cottage cheese in a bowl and stir in the chopped herbs. Cover lightly and set aside.

2 Cut the peeled bell peppers into thin strips and set aside. Cut the melon in half, discard the seeds and cut into small wedges.

3 Arrange the salad greens on a large serving platter with the melon wedges.

4 Spoon the herb-flavored cottage cheese on the platter and arrange the reserved bell peppers, the grapes, and red onion slices on the platter.

5 To make the dressing, mix the lime juice, chile, honey, and soy sauce together in a small bowl or pitcher, then drizzle over the salad and serve.

avocado, tomato & mozzarella salad

serves 4
- 2 tbsp pine nuts
- 6 oz/175 g dried fusilli (pasta spirals)
- 6 tomatoes
- 8 oz/225 g mozzarella cheese
- 1 large avocado
- 2 tbsp lemon juice
- 3 tbsp chopped fresh basil, plus extra sprigs to garnish
- salt and pepper

dressing
- 6 tbsp extra virgin olive oil
- 2 tbsp white wine vinegar
- 1 tsp whole-grain mustard
- pinch of sugar
- salt and pepper

1 Spread the pine nuts out onto a baking sheet and toast under a preheated hot broiler for 1–2 minutes. Remove and let cool. Bring a large pan of lightly salted water to a boil over medium heat. Add the pasta and cook for 8–10 minutes, or according to the package directions, until tender but still firm to the bite. Drain the pasta thoroughly and refresh in cold water. Drain again and let cool.

2 Thinly slice the tomatoes and the mozzarella cheese. Using a sharp knife, cut the avocado in half, then remove the pit and skin. Cut into thin slices lengthwise and sprinkle with lemon juice to prevent discoloration. To make the dressing, whisk the oil, vinegar, mustard, and sugar together in a small bowl. Season to taste with salt and pepper.

3 Arrange the tomatoes, mozzarella cheese, and avocado alternately in overlapping slices on a large serving plate. Toss the pasta with half the dressing and the chopped basil, and season to taste with salt and pepper. Spoon the pasta onto the plate and pour over the remaining dressing. Sprinkle over the pine nuts and garnish with fresh basil sprigs. Serve immediately.

arugula & parmesan salad with pine nuts

serves 4

- 2 handfuls of arugula leaves
- 1 small fennel bulb
- 5 tbsp olive oil
- 2 tbsp balsamic vinegar
- 3½ oz/100 g Parmesan cheese
- ⅓ cup pine nuts
- salt and pepper

1 Wash the arugula, discarding any wilted leaves or coarse stems, and pat dry. Divide among 4 serving plates. Halve the fennel bulb and slice it finely. Arrange the sliced fennel over the arugula.

2 Whisk together the oil and vinegar with salt and pepper to taste. Drizzle a little of the dressing over each serving. Shave the Parmesan cheese thinly using a knife or vegetable peeler.

3 Toast the pine nuts in a dry skillet until golden brown. Top the salad with the Parmesan cheese shavings and toasted pine nuts. Serve immediately.

three - color salad

serves 4
- 10 oz/280 g mozzarella cheese, drained
- 8 plum tomatoes
- 20 fresh basil leaves
- ½ cup extra virgin olive oil
- salt and pepper

1 Cut the mozzarella into thin slices. Cut the tomatoes into thin slices.

2 Arrange the cheese and tomato slices on 4 individual serving plates and season to taste with salt. Set aside in a cool place for 30 minutes.

3 Sprinkle the basil leaves over the salad, then drizzle with the oil and season with pepper to taste. Serve immediately.

asparagus & tomato salad

serves 4

- 8 oz/225 g asparagus spears
- 1 handful mâche
- 1 handful arugula or mizuna leaves
- 1 lb/450 g ripe tomatoes, sliced
- 12 black olives, pitted and chopped
- 1 tbsp toasted pine nuts

dressing

- 1 tsp lemon oil
- 1 tbsp olive oil
- 1 tsp whole-grain mustard
- 2 tbsp balsamic vinegar
- salt and pepper

1 Steam the asparagus spears for 8 minutes, or until tender. Rinse under cold running water to prevent them from cooking any further, then cut into 2-inch/5-cm pieces.

2 Arrange the mâche and arugula around a salad platter to form the base of the salad. Then place the sliced tomatoes and asparagus on the platter.

3 Sprinkle the black olives and pine nuts over the top. To make the dressing, place all the ingredients in a screw-top jar and shake vigorously until they are well blended. Drizzle over the salad and serve.

watercress, mint & zucchini salad

serves 4
- 2 zucchini, cut into sticks
- 1 cup chopped green beans
- 1 green bell pepper, seeded and cut into strips
- 2 celery stalks, sliced
- 1 bunch watercress
- salt

dressing
- scant 1 cup plain yogurt
- 1 garlic clove, crushed
- 2 tbsp chopped fresh mint
- pepper

1 Bring a saucepan of lightly salted water to a boil, add the zucchini batons and green beans, and cook for 5 minutes. Drain, rinse under cold running water, and drain again. Set aside to cool completely.

2 Mix the zucchini and green beans with the bell pepper strips, celery, and watercress in a large serving bowl.

3 To make the dressing, mix the dressing ingredients together in a separate bowl.

4 Spoon the dressing onto the salad and serve immediately.

minted pea
& melon salad

serves 4
- 1 large wedge watermelon
- ½ small honeydew melon
- ½ Charentais or cantaloupe melon
- ½ cucumber, peeled and diced
- 1 cup fresh pea shoots
- fresh mint leaves, to garnish

dressing
- 3 tbsp light olive oil
- 1 tbsp white wine vinegar
- ½ tsp superfine sugar
- 1 tbsp chopped fresh mint
- salt and pepper

1 Cut the flesh from all the melons into even chunks, removing any seeds. Put the chunks into a bowl with the cucumber.

2 To make the dressing, whisk the dressing ingredients together in a separate bowl.

3 Pour the dressing over the melons and cucumber and toss well to coat. Cover and chill for 1 hour.

4 Add the pea shoots to the chilled melons and cucumber and gently toss together. Transfer to a serving bowl and serve garnished with mint leaves.

green & white bean salad

serves 4
- ½ cup dried cannellini beans, soaked overnight and drained
- 8 oz/225 g fine green beans, trimmed
- ½ red onion, thinly sliced
- 12 pitted black olives
- 1 tbsp snipped fresh chives

dressing
- ½ tbsp lemon juice
- ½ tsp Dijon mustard
- 6 tbsp extra virgin olive oil
- salt and pepper

1 Place the cannellini beans in a large saucepan. Cover with cold water and bring to a boil. Boil rapidly for 15 minutes, then reduce the heat and simmer for an additional 30 minutes, or until tender. Drain and set aside.

2 Meanwhile, plunge the green beans into a large pan of boiling water. Bring back to a boil and cook for 4 minutes, until just tender but still brightly colored. Drain and set aside.

3 Whisk together the dressing ingredients, seasoning with salt and pepper to taste, then let stand. While both types of beans are still slightly warm, turn them into a shallow serving dish.

4 Scatter over the onion, olives, and chives. Whisk the dressing again and spoon over the salad. Serve at room temperature.

red pepper & radicchio salad

serves 4

- 2 red bell peppers
- 1 head radicchio, separated into leaves
- 4 cooked whole beets, cut into matchsticks
- 12 radishes, sliced
- 4 scallions, finely chopped
- 4 tbsp vinaigrette
- fresh crusty bread, to serve

1 Core and seed the bell peppers and slice into rounds.

2 Arrange the radicchio leaves in a salad bowl. Add the bell pepper, beets, radishes, and scallions. Drizzle with the vinaigrette and serve with crusty bread.

marinated pepper salad

serves 4

- 2 red bell peppers
- 2 yellow bell peppers
- 1 red onion, coarsely chopped
- 2 garlic cloves, chopped
- 6 tbsp olive oil
- 1 cup drained, marinated black olives
- 3½ oz/100 g mini mozzarella balls, drained
- 2 tbsp coarsely torn, fresh basil leaves
- 2 tbsp balsamic vinegar
- salt and pepper

1 Preheat the oven to 375°F/190°C. Halve the bell peppers lengthwise, keeping the stalks on. Remove the seeds and white membrane Put the bell peppers, cut-side uppermost, into a shallow roasting pan. Sprinkle with the onion and garlic, season with salt and pepper, and drizzle with half of the olive oil. Roast for 40 minutes, until the bell peppers are tender. Let cool.

2 Put the cold bell peppers on a serving plate and pour any juices left in the roasting pan over them. Sprinkle with the olives, mozzarella balls, and basil.

3 Whisk together the remaining olive oil and the balsamic vinegar and pour the mixture over the bell peppers. Cover and let marinate in the refrigerator for at least 2 hours (or overnight) before serving.

pasta salad
with bell peppers

serves 4

- 1 red bell pepper
- 1 orange bell pepper
- 10 oz/280 g dried conchiglie (pasta shells)
- 5 tbsp extra virgin olive oil
- 2 tbsp lemon juice
- 2 tbsp green pesto
- 1 garlic clove, finely chopped
- 3 tbsp shredded fresh basil leaves
- salt and pepper

1 Preheat the broiler. Put the whole bell peppers on a baking sheet and place under the hot broiler, turning frequently, for 15 minutes, or until charred all over. Remove with tongs and place in a bowl. Cover with crumpled paper towels and reserve.

2 Meanwhile, bring a large saucepan of lightly salted water to a boil. Add the pasta, return to a boil, and cook for 8–10 minutes, or according to the package directions, until tender.

3 Combine the olive oil, lemon juice, pesto, and garlic in a bowl, whisking well to mix. Drain the pasta, add it to the pesto mixture while still hot, and toss well. Reserve.

4 When the bell peppers are cool enough to handle, peel off the skins, then cut open and remove the seeds. Chop the flesh coarsely and add to the pasta with the basil. Season to taste with salt and pepper and toss well. Serve.

roasted vegetable salad

serves 4
- 1 onion
- 1 eggplant,
  about 8 oz/225 g
- 1 red bell pepper, seeded
- 1 orange bell pepper,
  seeded
- 1 large zucchini,
  about 6 oz/175 g
- 2–4 garlic cloves
- 2–4 tbsp olive oil
- 1 tbsp shredded fresh basil
- salt and pepper
- freshly shaved Parmesan
  cheese and fresh crusty
  bread, to serve

dressing
- 1 tbsp balsamic vinegar
- 2 tbsp extra virgin olive oil

1 Preheat the oven to 400°F/200°C. Cut all the vegetables into even-size wedges, put into a roasting pan, and sprinkle over the garlic.

2 Pour over 2 tablespoons of the olive oil and turn the vegetables in the oil until well coated. Add a little salt and pepper. Roast in the preheated oven for 40 minutes, or until tender, adding the extra olive oil if becoming too dry.

3 To make the dressing, place the ingredients in a screw-top jar and shake vigorously until they are well blended.

4 Once the vegetables are cooked, remove from the oven, arrange on a serving dish, and pour over the dressing. Sprinkle with the basil. Serve with Parmesan cheese and fresh crusty bread.

red cabbage & beet salad

serves 4
- 3¾ cups finely shredded red cabbage
- 1 cup julienned cooked beet
- 1 apple, cored and thinly sliced
- 1 tbsp lemon juice
- 1 tbsp sunflower seeds
- 1 tbsp pumpkin seeds
- salt and pepper

dressing
- 3 tbsp mayonnaise
- 2 tbsp Greek-style yogurt
- 1 tbsp red wine vinegar

1 Put the cabbage, beet, and apple slices into a large bowl. Add the lemon juice and mix well.

2 To make the dressing, mix the dressing ingredients together in a separate bowl. Pour the dressing over the salad and stir well. Season with salt and pepper, cover, and chill in the refrigerator for at least 1 hour.

3 Stir the salad thoroughly and adjust the seasoning to taste. Sprinkle with the sunflower and pumpkin seeds just before serving.

beet, fennel & avocado salad

serves 4–6

- 2 avocados, halved, pitted, and thinly sliced
- 2 fennel bulbs, trimmed and thinly sliced
- 2 golden, striped, or ruby cooked beets, peeled and thinly sliced
- 2 tbsp snipped chives
- 2 tbsp finely chopped fresh parsley
- 1 tbsp finely shredded fresh basil
- 1 tbsp finely chopped fresh mint
- ⅓ cup grated ricotta salata cheese

dressing

- ½ cup sunflower oil
- 2 tbsp fresh orange juice
- salt and pepper

1 To make the dressing, put the oil and orange juice in a large, nonmetallic bowl and whisk until blended. Add salt and pepper to taste.

2 Add the avocado and fennel to the bowl and toss with your hands to coat in the dressing. (At this point the salad can be covered with plastic wrap and chilled for up to 4 hours.)

3 When ready to serve, arrange the beet slices on a serving platter or individual plates. Add the herbs to the bowl with the fennel and avocado and toss together. Stir the cheese into the bowl and toss again, then mound the salad on top of the beet slices, and serve.

potato salad

serves 4

- 1 lb 9 oz/700 g new potatoes
- 8 scallions
- 1 cup mayonnaise
- 1 tsp paprika
- salt and pepper
- 2 tbsp snipped fresh chives and a pinch of paprika, to garnish

1 Bring a large pan of lightly salted water to a boil. Add the potatoes and cook for 10–15 minutes, or until just tender.

2 Drain the potatoes and rinse them under cold running water until completely cold. Drain again. Transfer the potatoes to a bowl and reserve until required.

3 Using a sharp knife, slice the scallions thinly on the diagonal.

4 Mix the mayonnaise, paprika, and salt and pepper to taste together in a bowl. Pour the mixture over the potatoes. Add the scallions to the potatoes and toss together.

5 Transfer the potato salad to a serving bowl and garnish with snipped chives and a pinch of paprika. Cover and let chill in the refrigerator until required.

wild rice salad

serves 4
- 1⅓ cups wild rice
- 3½ cups water
- 1 red bell pepper, skinned, seeded, and thinly sliced
- 1 yellow bell pepper, skinned, seeded, and thinly sliced
- 1 orange bell pepper, skinned, seeded, and thinly sliced
- ½ cucumber, halved lengthwise and sliced
- 1 orange, peeled, pith removed, and cubed
- 3 ripe tomatoes, cut into chunks
- 1 red onion, finely chopped
- generous handful chopped fresh flat-leaf parsley

dressing
- 1 clove garlic, crushed
- 1 tbsp balsamic vinegar
- 2 tbsp extra virgin olive oil
- salt and pepper

1 Put the wild rice and water into a large pan and bring to a boil. Stir, then cover and simmer for 40 minutes, or until the rice is tender but still firm to the bite. Uncover the rice for the last few minutes of cooking to let any excess water evaporate.

2 To make the dressing, place all the ingredients in a screw-top jar and shake vigorously until they are well blended.

3 Drain the rice and turn into a large bowl. Pour over the dressing and mix in. Then mix in the chopped bell peppers, cucumber, orange, tomatoes, red onion, and flat-leaf parsley and serve.

chile spiced paneer salad

serves 2

- 6 tbsp sunflower oil
- 8 oz/225 g paneer, cubed
- 1 tsp mustard seeds
- 1 tsp ground cumin
- 1 garlic clove, crushed
- 1 small green chile, seeded and finely chopped
- 3 cups scallions, finely chopped
- 3 cups baby salad greens

tomato chutney

- 2 ripe tomatoes, peeled, seeded, and diced
- 1 shallot, finely chopped
- 2 tbsp sunflower oil
- 2 tsp lemon juice
- 1 tbsp chopped fresh cilantro
- salt and pepper

1 To make the tomato chutney, mix the ingredients together in a bowl. Chill in the refrigerator for 30 minutes.

2 Heat the oil in a large skillet. Add the paneer cubes and cook over medium–high heat, turning frequently, for 4–5 minutes, until golden brown all over (be careful because the oil may spit). Remove the paneer with a slotted spoon and drain on paper towels.

3 Carefully pour off half the hot oil from the skillet. Add the mustard seeds and ground cumin to the remaining oil and fry for a few seconds. Stir in the garlic, chile, and scallions and cook for 1–2 minutes. Return the paneer to the skillet and toss to coat well in the spicy mixture.

4 Divide the salad greens between 2 serving plates. Top with the hot paneer. Spoon the tomato chutney over it and serve immediately.

Index